Bugging Out

By

David E Crossley

Index

Introduction

Bug Out, evacuate, get out of dodge, head for the hills: everybody knows the terms and whenever Preppers or Survivalists gather on or off line it is a topic that can occupy conversation for hours. Perhaps only discussion of which knife, or bivvy, or torch, or whatever, should be in the pack you grab on your way out occupies more of their time and mental energy than the concept itself.

For many of the Prepper community, Bug Out is the basic concept and the default option. The plans that they carefully formulate, examine and in some cases practise, often don't seem to feature any alternative, and yet, for the majority of emergencies, staying home is actually a much more sensible choice. Information on what you need for that eventuality is covered in Bugging In, the companion volume to this book.

Ideally, your normal home would be the perfect retreat you would want to head for if you had to evacuate from somewhere else. Unfortunately for most people that ideal simply isn't practical, for reasons of cost or work or other requirements of everyday life.

But supposing you did live there, even then there is always the risk of a situation occurring where bugging out to somewhere else is the only sensible thing to do. If your house is on fire, or being threatened by fast-approaching flames from somewhere else, then a rapid exit in a safe direction is clearly the way to go.

So the concept of Bugging Out has merit under various circumstances but what we should consider is that it is not as simple as the salesmen of pre-packed 72 hour kits might like to make out. There are in fact many things affecting whether, where, when, and how you should go, what you should have ready to take with you if you do, and how you survive when you are out there.

The 72 hour concept came from the fact that if a major

emergency affects a limited area, the government and emergency services will respond but it takes them a while to get organised and deploy. Unfortunately, if the area affected is large rather than local and especially if your neighbourhood isn't a priority, they might never arrive and then it is all down to you.

The following chapters will hopefully help you to make the right choices in regard to what you need to prepare and the things you need to do to be ready for when those situations arise.

Whether to go

In essence, the answer to this seems fairly simple: you go if that will be safer for you and your family/group than it is to stay. However, the factors that go into that decision are not necessarily so straight forward.

Firstly, there might be a moral dimension; perhaps you have dependents who for health and mobility reasons cannot or will not go and who you will not leave behind. They could be relatives, or you might be a public employee or volunteer and unwilling to abandon your duty. Ultimately, whether you stay may not make any difference to their fate, but if it gives them comfort in the last hours or minutes, then to you that might be enough reason to do so, whatever the risk to yourself. Some people would say that risking two lives instead of one in such a way is foolish; you may differ. Whether it is from soldiers supporting their comrades in battle or civilians in many other situations, there are inspiring examples of this type of courage and dedication in every disaster.

Next there is the calculation of the risks where you are, compared to those that exist where you intend to go and on the journey to get there. This does depend on the situation; if you are facing imminent and irreducible threats that do not exist elsewhere then the only realistic survival option is to leave but under other circumstances it isn't so clear cut. What do you do, for example, if your current situation is dire, but you don't know that anywhere else you could get to would be any better?

So what situations might force you to flee from your home? A look at the news over the years would give us a depressingly long list of things that have done that for millions of people, though far fewer thankfully in the UK. Some of these happen almost annually in some countries, others more rarely.

In the UK the list includes:

Flood
Fire – accidental
Fire – arson
Storm damage
Subsidence and landslip
Industrial accident
Terrorism

Internationally you could add:
War
Famine
Pandemic
Tornado
Hurricane
Civil war and banditry
Tsunami
Drought
Earthquake
Volcanic activity
Radiation release
Chemical release

Some items on the international list have actually affected UK too; in some cases not for many years, in others much more recently.

In 2007 Hurricane force winds killed 11 people and damaged many homes

In 2006 a tornado in London killed 1 person and caused £10 million of damage

In 2005 a tornado in Birmingham UK injured 30 and caused £40million pounds of damage including complete destruction of some homes.

In 2005 a series of explosions at the Buncefield oil storage depot, Hertfordshire devastated the terminal and many surrounding properties. There were no fatalities but damages accounted to £750 million.

In 1990 winds of up to 100mph killed 97 people and cause £3.37 BILLION of damage across the UK

In 1987 Michael Fish's famous non-hurricane killed 18 people, wrecked houses and blocked roads

Fortunately, we haven't seen people forced from their homes in UK due to war since 1945 and not because of famine or pandemic for over 100 years but of course those events have happened in the UK in the past, as have powerful earthquakes, the most recent of which in 1884 destroyed over 1200 buildings in Colchester, Essex. It is possible any of these could happen again.

Of the more recent events, flooding has undoubtedly been the major cause of evacuation, with direct or indirect damage, e.g. falling trees, caused by high winds a close second. In addition, 45,000 homes were affected by domestic fires in 2011 and many others (no full statistics available) evacuated due to threat of the fire spreading, or noxious smoke or chemical fumes, from some of the 25,000 industrial fires attended by the Fire Service in England and Wales. Tenants also had to flee from their homes when shops, banks and pubs were set alight by rioters. In 2012 homes had to be abandoned when the land around them collapsed because of erosion.

Outside the UK but affecting some British citizens, in New Orleans 2005 as Hurricane Katrina closed in, the residents of low lying areas had no option but to leave. In New York 2012 as Hurricane Sandy approached people were ordered out of some areas on the waterfront. Despite this, as always happens, some residents stayed for any of several reasons. Some of them died as a result.

Although these are not the 'head for the hills' events that many Preppers think of when they talk about bugging out, they are in fact relatively common occurrences that do force people to relocate. Sometimes that move is temporary; sometimes the devastation is so complete they have nothing left to which they can return. These events can happen to any of us, anywhere in the UK or when we are abroad, and cost the unprepared the loss of everything they own and major inconvenience.

However, they are Bug Out situations for which the decision to leave is relatively easy and, as we will examine later, for which it is simple and inexpensive to prepare.

If the scientists who are predicting climate change are correct, or the financial crises now affecting much of the world progress to a true depression, or a pandemic does hit, or terrorists strike a financial or commercial centre with a chemical or radiological dirty bomb, some pundits foresee a social collapse with associated loss of governmental control, and law and order.

In many ways, improved technology has made our lives seem more secure. Communications and transport are generally far more reliable in settled times. However, the interconnected nature of international commerce, and particularly of the supply chain, means that any major disruption of those communications, or of fuel supplies required for transport, or of financial infrastructure, makes us extremely vulnerable because of our reliance on imported food and other goods. The UK is not even close to being self-sufficient in most of the essentials and with our growing population is becoming ever less so. Other parts of Europe have already seen food riots (as well as political/economic ones) in the cities as a result of their financial problems. Are they really less likely here if we were hit by a major disruption in our supplies?

Even then the idea that most people would flee from the cities and head out into the countryside is not borne out by historical precedent in most cases. For a start people do not all realise or accept the need to leave at the same time. Many will be city born and reared, with no confidence in their ability to function in the wilds. Remember that, although some children were evacuated, people did not abandon the cities even when they were being bombed daily during the Second World War.

Until they see an immediate and undeniable personal threat, most people are slow to leave the home and possessions for which they have worked so hard.

In some situations, such as civil war, drought, famine, or economic collapse, people actually tend to head to the cities, and particularly the Capital, where they expect governmental control to be stronger and work or aid easier to come by. This is what happened during the last great depression and has done in parts of Africa such as Somalia and Ethiopia, where shanty towns and large refugee camps have grown around the major cities and where international aid agencies concentrate most of their efforts.

Those camps would not be there unless things were pretty bad outside, but nevertheless, unless civil unrest, banditry or other conditions make it unviable, if you have made careful preparations including a secure place to go, this ingress of refugees might signal that it is in fact time for you to leave. The resources of the city will inevitably be stretched. Conditions will deteriorate and both disease and crime increase. If something stops the supply of aid to the camps, you would have a huge number of desperate angry people looking to take what they need from anyone they suspect might have it and at any cost. You wouldn't want to be there when that happened.

Although they are perhaps less likely, there are also some other potential disasters that could cause a widespread evacuation. One or more ground burst nuclear explosions with resultant down-wind fallout, caused by either terrorists or a rogue state, or a nuclear power station meltdown such as the ones at Chernobyl or Fukushima, or an industrial chemical release on the scale of Bhopal, could force people to flee from the affected area. A pandemic with extremely high fatality rate could make conditions in the cities unbearable for most of the survivors.

These, along with things such as invasion, or the imposition of a dictatorship or police state, are the scenarios most often proposed as the main reasons for a general Bug Out. Note though, that except for the last three, most would still only affect a restricted area and perhaps only masses of decaying and unburied dead would result in a Bug Out from cities across the whole nation. If you are caught in an area affected by one of the more limited Events, however, bugging out might well be your best or only survival option.

So to summarise; in making the decision whether to leave you should consider:

1.   Are the reasons to go greater than those to stay?

2.   Do you have somewhere to go that offers greater security and resources than where you are?

3.   Do you have a reasonable chance of safely getting to your destination?

Where to go

One of the first steps you should take after making the decision to prepare for emergencies is to identify the list of crises you believe might realistically affect you. In the previous chapter I listed those that have happened in the past in the UK that might cause you to Bug Out. However, not all of those are necessarily a threat to YOU. For example, you might live part way up a well drained hill on very stable ground, so that you do not consider flooding or subsidence to be a problem for you. On the other hand you might be in an urban area with a large chemical plant not far away and put that high on your list.

In the companion book – Bugging In – to this volume, you will find a chapter on Risk Assessment and Survival Planning that explains how to identify and evaluate these factors.

Identifying the threats is important because they could also affect what features you look for in places you consider as BOLs. Those locations should be safe from the differing threats in so far as possible but if you aren't going to have to leave home because of flood then one that might possibly be affected by that danger at other times but is far enough away to be clear of any chemical leak now, could still be an option.

You would have to be very unlucky to face two disasters at the same time, though it does happen. Consider New York during Hurricane Sandy when winds caused damage, a storm surge washed houses away, large areas were flooded, electrical short circuits started fires that ravaged hundreds of homes, and looting became a problem in some areas, with many of those occurring simultaneously! So choose your BOLs carefully and have a number of back-ups open to you.

When a disaster strikes, the unexpected nature of the event, and lack of reliable and accurate information, is bound to cause anxiety and confusion.

Without preparation this could lead to panic, some of the

features of which include: faulty decision making, forgetfulness, uncoordinated and unhelpful activity, or in some cases, metal paralysis with an inability to make decisions or do anything productive at all.

Mental and physical preparation gives confidence and helps to avoid panic. Knowing where you are going when you leave greatly reduces stress and improves logical decision making, substantially increasing your chances of survival. Knowing that you are going to have the things you will need when you get there is even better. Knowing that all of this is because YOU recognised the dangers, made the decisions and did the work to be prepared, should be cause for a huge pat on the back and a welcome boost to your morale!

As part of those preps you should think about the several options of where you could go, including:

Official refugee shelter or camp
Local/charity shelter
Family
Friends
Hotel or B&B
Your place of work
Urban site
Caravan/motorhome - static or mobile
Boat
Camp site - with your own tent, etc or with huts/cabins
Wilderness location

Which of these are available to you and which you might choose depends on the nature of the Event, and in particular whether it is personal, local, or widespread. After considering some general points we will look at the features, benefits and drawbacks for each of them.

In preparing in case you need a BOL, you should in fact select not one but several places, in differing directions from your home and at differing distances, so that you have choices for whichever direction the threat comes from and for both local and wide area emergencies.

Information on emergency response, including identified official shelter locations, should be available on the website of regional and local government authorities and in particular in the pages of the Emergency Planning Department.

You probably know or can quickly identify the more local places that might be used for refugees; such as churches, village halls, schools and Scout huts. Other types of BOL you will have to seek out for yourself.

When choosing a BOL you should consider:

Routes to and from - will you be able to get to it in the event of an emergency e.g. is it accessible using routes not likely to be blocked by other evacuees or structural failures?

Area - Is it less likely to attract other people because its advantages are not obvious to the uninformed and it is off the main transport routes or easily accessed alternatives?

Features - Does it have the facilities you might need e.g. supplies/foraging/water/allies/etc and will it provide protection from expected disasters e.g. on high ground if for relocation from flood, the other side of water or a motorway if you are fleeing from an area fire?

Structure - Will you be able to access it? Does it offer sound shelter and security?

Where possible, you might also want to establish a cache at your BOLs, to supplement things you take with you, or replace items you didn't have chance to collect before leaving or which you have lost on the way. Within these you could include items particularly useful at that location e.g. fishing kit by a lake or river, snares near a rabbit warren, a crowbar and hacksaw near a food store, etc.

Family or friends might find space for a bag or box that

you leave with them. At some BOLs, and various places en-route if the journey is a long one, you might bury a container of equipment and supplies. Later in the book we will examine appropriate sites, containers and contents for caches.

In all cases, you will want to investigate what resources are available in the vicinity of the BOL, so that you can forage, and around some you could extend those resources by indulging in Guerrilla Gardening, by planting edible or medicinal plants in wild areas where they do not occur naturally.

These supplemental supplies will provide a palpable bonus to the skills and knowledge you can provide, to help ensure that you are seen by residents and locals as a benefit rather than a burden at your new home.

Where appropriate you should visit potential BOLs often and offer help or participate in activities there, so that you become known as a friendly face and are more likely to be greeted with a welcome instead of a rejection.

After you have established your locations you should discretely check them on a regular basis, in order to ensure that there have been no changes in the area that make one no longer viable. If that happens, find an alternative as soon as possible. Check too that caches have not been discovered or disturbed but do this even more discretely. Replace with another in a different place any that have been compromised.

A suitable selection of pre-established BOLs is a major and potentially critical part of your preps, and can provide a huge boost to morale, security and comfort when it is most needed but a BOL that you can't get to, can't access if you do, or which doesn't provide the things you need when you get there, isn't a useful part of the plan.

Official refugee shelters or camps

Many Survivalists and Preppers have a golden rule; 'Never become a refugee!' They recognise that there might be a need to Bug Out, but there is an essential difference in the mindset of the two methodologies.

Someone who bugs out does so independently, making their own decisions on where, when and how they go, and with the intention of providing for themselves. A refugee also leaves their normal place of residence, possibly independently or maybe on official transport, but with the intention of seeking official shelter and aid.

Most often, refugees will be directed or taken to an official shelter or camp. These will be set up with the basic facilities of shelter, water, food, hygiene, and medical care, and possibly minor comforts such as camp beds or foam pads and blankets.

They also give the authorities the thing they yearn for most above all, a sense of CONTROL. Government agencies and NGOs hate independent thinkers!

They should in fact appreciate the efforts of some people to look after themselves and accept that it helps everyone by aiding official efforts to target resources to those who truly need them, but almost invariably, when evacuating an area officials will do everything in their power to persuade or force people to follow the master plan.

In their eyes anyone who does their own thing is just a trouble maker who will get in the way of efficient operations, however inefficient and inept those operations might actually turn out to be.

This attitude also carries over into the shelters. On arrival, refugees will be recorded, sometimes allocated a numbered badge or label, and either asked or compelled to hand over any food, drink, or other resources they might have that could be added to the stockpile, 'for the good of all'. In particular, the officials running the shelter will try to confiscate all alcohol, some medicines, or anything that could even possibly be used as a weapon.

They will also ask for details of any injuries, sickness, or disability. This might lead to welcome medical treatment, or it could be a precursor to isolation and triage. You may be asked to fill in a form, in which case until you hand it in duly completed you will not get the number or chits or whatever that you will have to give in exchange for food and other necessities, though if you have difficulties filling in the form someone would usually go through the questions and fill it in for you.

In some shelters families are allowed to stay together, though in others I have seen, males over the age of puberty are separated from the women and younger children.

Amenities are usually very basic and when, as often happens, the numbers of refugees taken in exceed the capacity to cope of the officials, volunteers and facilities - particularly toilets and other hygiene resources – things become grim.

In addition, you lose any of the privacy and self-determination you would usually enjoy. The noises, smells, activities and habits of those crowded around you become all pervasive. Thefts, arguments and fights are common, rape less so because of the public nature of most venues but always something to guard against if there is anywhere it could happen.

Some places become bitterly cold, others far too hot due to the number of people in too small a space. Sleep, or even adequate rest, is difficult, discomfort the norm. All this is on top of the stress, anxiety and sense of loss you will have suffered from the original Event.

Almost all these conditions also apply to larger camps. You

might have a bit more space and privacy, and the noises and smells will come from a yard or two away rather than feet or inches. Some camps will provide basic cooking equipment and supplies rather than communal feeding, but in those cases the supplies tend to be even more basic and repetitive. The downsides come from the larger area and number of people.

Large camps and large numbers of people are correspondingly more difficult to control. In many, cliques or gangs form, sometimes based around the areas of the camp in which people find themselves, in others groups with some shared factor, such as religion, ethnicity, previous location, etc, gather into the same part of camp, often driving out those not of their clan in the process. Unless a force with sufficient authority and strength steps in to impose order, organised inter-group crime and violence then develops.

In all, if your idea of organised shelters comes from old video footage of people in underground stations having a merry sing song, then for a more realistic view research instead the recent examples in Africa, Asia, and even North America.

Local and charity shelters

The effectiveness of local and charity shelters varies widely. Generally they are less officious and more caring, but less well equipped and provisioned than state run refuges.

I passed through a church in a war-torn area of Europe, with over two hundred people crammed inside lying on the pews and stone floors. The one toilet in the building was blocked and overflowing, so that the graveyard outside had become the communal latrine for both bodily waste functions, without any organisation of where people relieved themselves. There was no source of food or other supplies for the refugees and the church candles hardly raised the temperature above freezing.

Care for the wounded came mainly from their relatives. There was one nurse among them, but with no equipment, medication or supplies there wasn't much she could do beyond that offered by family members and confirm when someone was beyond resuscitation. The priest did occasionally manage to rouse some to their knees for prayer, or to their feet for hymns, particularly when the shelling drew close, but it was not a place that offered much hope or comfort beyond that inspired by faith.

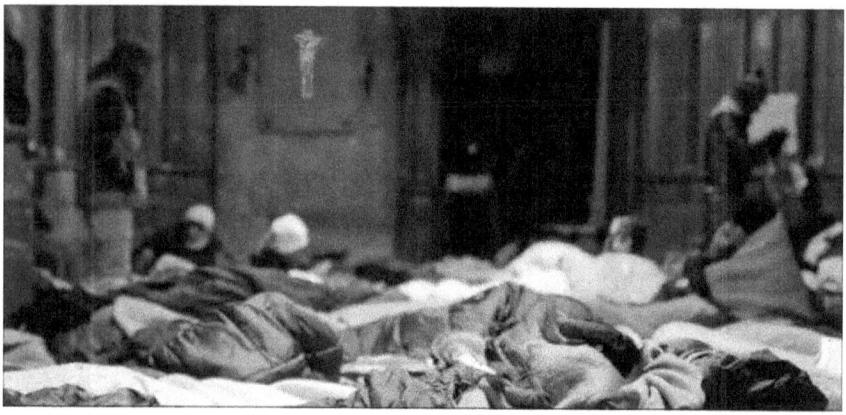

Then again, I have worked in centres that were run efficiently by volunteers who seemed to have a sometimes confusingly optimistic and endlessly cheerful character. Groups such as the Red Cross volunteers, Women's Institute, and others often have training, practise, and experience with shelters and a good supply of equipment with which to operate and are accustomed to cooperating with other similar organisations and the main emergency services.

Being local, they also often have members who are, or have contacts with, farmers or managers of large retail stores, on which they can call most persuasively for support. They do tend to operate for relatively limited numbers, and the people they are aiding are also usually local, so there is a bond that can be very reassuring and eliminates much of the hostility found in larger shelters. Even these worthy groups do vary in their capability though, depending largely on the quality of leadership and level of experience of their more senior members.

Some of these smaller, independent shelters can offer advantages over the large official ones, but in others the conditions are even worse. All things considered, you would still be far better off relying on your own skills, knowledge and preparations, than you would hoping to find one of the good ones.

Family and Friends

At first this seems an obvious choice, but is it for you?

In my case, my wife and I live in central Scotland, near Glasgow. We have a daughter who lives in Germany and a son in Leicester, but that isn't a suitable BOL for various reasons. I have two sisters. One lives near Torquay, Devon, the other in Australia. The Event that caused us to Bug Out would have to be wide ranging indeed to make the homes of any of those family members viable BOLs for us.

We also have family who live up on the Moray Firth. It is about 150 miles to the north east of us but gives us a viable longer range potential BOL in that direction.

There are a couple of close neighbours to whom we might go if the event was very personal e.g. a fire pretty much confined our house, but they are close enough that if the effects were any wider than that the chances are that they would be leaving too.

We have other friends we could turn to, but most are almost as far away as my sister on the south coast; and the one nearest is by Manchester.

So although family and friends might automatically come to mind if you are planning for a Bug Out, you cannot take for granted that they offer a suitable place to go. Even if the distance is right you should compare their locality and area against the list of considerations given earlier in this chapter.

Don't look at their location through rose tinted glasses. Consider their place as you would if it was inhabited by strangers.

If one of their homes then does present as a good option, give serious thought to establishing a cache there, and to developing their mindset as Preppers too. That way they are prepped when you arrive and can also leave a cache with you in case the transfer is the other way around. If the Event is wide reaching and either of you does not survive, or does but cannot reach the other, the extra resources might be a very welcome gift for your friends.

Now, believe me, I know how strong the draw is to be with family and/or good friends after a traumatic event, but if you are serious about survival you MUST make these decisions logically. It is easier to do that when there is no pressure from a looming disaster. If something does happen, then before you move reassess the location in light of the situation that is making you evacuate.

If in that case it is still a safe option for this emergency, then consider the fact that you will have good people to be with as a bonus.

Hotels and B&Bs

 After you are clear of the immediately affected disaster area, hotels and B&Bs offer a lot of advantages as BOLs, provided you can pay for them. In more destructive Events even abandoned places often still hold useful resources in rooms and cleaners' cupboards after the obvious parts such as kitchen and bar have been looted.

Commercial accommodation will provide comfort,

security, communications, privacy when you want it, catering, and a supply of toiletries and other essentials.

If you fled with not much more than you were wearing (which shouldn't happen if you apply the advice in this book!) they can be a real oasis of relief. If you intend to take pets, make sure the hotel will accept them.

If the emergency has had effects beyond your very local area, the hotel and their suppliers might face some shortages but if you have some preps in reserve you can continue to take advantage of the other facilities for as long as the place remains open.

However, another prep you might need is a supply of cash. While some hotels may have retained a manual billing system for using credit or debit cards others will not, and some B&Bs will never have had such an arrangement. If mains electricity or networks are down they will not be able to use electronic billing systems and nor will you be able to draw from an ATM. Some might accept a cheque but that is another system on its way out. So a sensible prep for either a Bug In or Bug Out situation is to keep enough cash on hand to cover your needs for as long as is reasonable for you but at least a few days and preferably a couple of weeks as a minimum.

Something else to bear in mind is that this type of accommodation is familiar and psychologically comfortable for most people, so demand will be high. The key is to either get in early or be prepared to travel further or wider than the competition. Mid-range establishments will be full first, with the more expensive and the least desirable ends of the market getting more custom as they become all that is left, by which time prices in both will be rising.

Older and larger buildings potentially offer another feature and it is something you should check out. During the 1970s and 80s when I was doing a lot of travelling, the Cold War sometimes became rather warmer than most people realised. I therefore located a number of stone built country-house type hotels around the places from which I operated and on the routes I most often drove.

One of the essential attributes for which I was looking, was that they had an underground cellar. Many of these older places do, whereas newer buildings often have an air-conditioned room where they keep the beer and wine. That is fine for booze but not much good as protection from radiation if what you are fleeing is a nuclear explosion or meltdown.

The ones I chose, I frequented regularly for dinner or drinks and weekend stays, to the extent that I developed a friendly, first name relationship with the managers and staff. I also directed conversation at the bar to news events, common enough in those days, which allowed me to reveal some knowledge that showed I would be useful if I ever turned up looking for shelter. .

If radiation is one of your concerns and older hotels are not available where you are looking for a BOL, try to find a very large one. It should have reinforced concrete construction with multiple floors and minimal ledges outside the rooms. Two of the factors that give protection from radiation are distance and shielding (the other is time). A room with 5 or more floors below and 5 or more above in such a building, outside the blast area of the explosion and on the opposite side from it, gives a high protective value.

Your Place of Work

Whether this is useful does, of course, depend on where you work! However, if you have access outside of normal working hours should you need it, your workplace offers the advantage of being familiar surroundings and therefore somewhat reassuring in an emergency. You will also know all its benefits such as: where the tea, coffee and biscuits are kept; which of your workmates keep a stash of goodies in their desk or locker; where the first aid kits are; the most comfortable seating areas where you could sleep for a while, and lots of other things.

Unless you work in a major retailer, jewellers shop, or bank, then a workplace is not likely to be a first choice for looters, so you should be fairly secure there.

To be sure, it probably doesn't offer many facilities that would invite you to stay there long term, and it might be so close to home that  it is too near to consider as a BOL, but this is somewhere you shouldn't overlook when thinking about potential sites.

I have been stuck due to bad weather or other events a couple of times when, although I could have made my way home if it had been a real priority, it made more sense to doss down at work for the night. That was much safer than battling through flooded roads in the dark and it worked out fine. One of the things that helped is that I always keep a small cache at my workplace if I can't park my car – which always contains emergency kit - outside. You should consider doing the same.

Urban sites

Other than those above, there are some other urban sites that have potential for use as BOLs in certain circumstances.

Our closest BOL is one of our garages. Our house in town is in a terrace. On the opposite side of the road and slightly uphill is a crescent of garages for the residents of the terrace. That garage is watertight and not used for the car because it is a 4x4 and won't fit. We use the garage for some storage but some of the things kept in there – unused cardboard moving boxes, rubber matting, cut-offs of carpet, a hammer and tacks, and other things - are selected to quickly add insulation to the roof, walls and floor, and with a pair of camp chairs and a folding table provide that in the event of, for example, a house fire we would have a place to which we could quickly relocate.

With the emergency gear that is kept in the car we could then camp out near to the house while we dealt with all the administration involved and removed any valuables to a safe place before the local trash came rummaging for whatever they could steal. One of our friends has kitted out the shed on his allotment in ready prepared fashion and calls it 'my urban log cabin'. He also wants to be by his vegetables and fruit in a crisis in case they attract the attention of thieves. Many of you will have a lockup, outbuilding or similar facility close by that might serve for the purpose.

If you have to move further away, but not out of town, there are other options. During the Second World War, stations of the underground system were used as air raid shelters and many of the same were designated as shelters during the cold war. The below ground floors of some shops and shopping centres were also considered suitable and some government buildings and office blocks were either built with purpose designed shelters or had basement areas modified for the role. Most of those have had the signs displaying their function removed and have become storage areas but they are still there if you can identify them.

There are also large, disused, run down or incomplete buildings in parts of most cities that offer potential shelter, at least on a temporary basis. For those for whom long distance travel is difficult or impractical these can offer an alternative closer to home.

Sewers are a hazardous but possible option but, depending on the type of emergency, roof tops might be better. Within and around many cities there are roundabouts, abandoned graveyards, wooded areas between the carriageways of motorways and trunk roads, large parks, and paths alongside canals or rivers that offer overgrown hiding places.

So not all BOLs have to be at a distance from your home,

and in fact you should have a variety planned at close, middle, and long distance to meet various needs.

Caravans and Motorhomes

My name is David, and I'm a … Caravanner! There, I've said it!

Whatever you think of caravans if you aren't a caravanner but you have been stuck behind one doing 35mph for miles driving down a country road, they are, in fact, very good potential BOLs.

A static or mobile caravan is, quite literally, a home from home. Whether you Bug Out driving/towing from your house  or travel to one parked at a fixed location, they offer all the facilities needed for independent living. Many people who have been flooded out of their house have been provided with caravan by their insurance company, to live in while the house is dried and repaired, and then accepted the offer to buy when they can move back in.

For hundreds of thousands of others they are the holiday venue of choice. Some diehards like my wife and I are regular users at any time of year, other owners store them away for the winter and then roll them out at Easter. But we always have the reassurance of knowing 'The 'Van' is there if needed.

When not in use, ours is stored in a barn on a farm that is one of our primary BOLs, about 200 miles to the south of our main home. The farm offers spring water and private drainage, a large solar panel array on the roof of one of the barns, a private wind turbine, and many other advantages. There are 9 other caravans stored there, and of the 10 owners 5 of us are Preppers with an agreement to RV at the farm if a situation arises that makes that sensible. We don't discuss prepping with the farmer but we do shoot together to control pigeon and rabbits, help out at harvest time and with anything that arises when we are at the farm and so on. It all helps.

Caravans do have their limitations: if sited outside they are vulnerable to damage in extreme weather, and offer hardly any protection from radiation, fire or other attack, but anything other than one of the big static caravans is, by design, mobile so it can be repositioned to take best advantage from protective features – such as buildings, walls, embankments, etc - and to take account of changing conditions.

They also all offer full facilities for living off-grid, by use of bottled gas, generator or 12v battery. The battery can be recharged using a solar panel array and if gas and fuel for the generator becomes unavailable the 'van still provides shelter and many comforts while you revert to old ways and cook outside.

New caravans are by no means cheap these days but many second-hand ones still are. If you decide that they offer you a useful advantage but you haven't owned one before, take an experienced friend with you when looking to buy. The main killer for a caravan is damp – which is expensive to repair and usually far worse than it looks, but there are other things to check too, such as the condition of the tyres and chassis, gas system and electrics. Caravans do not have to go through a yearly MOT, though the vehicle components of a motorhome do, so there is no official check of their roadworthiness or other condition. Buyer beware!

When choosing between a motorhome and a towed caravan there are several factors to take into consideration.

Both variants offer much the same facilities but unless you

go large motorhomes generally have less room, so storage space, bathrooms size, etc., tend to be more limited.

For a towed caravan you have a wide range of choices for the towing vehicle, which means you could choose a 4x4 with all the advantages that offers when you need them, whereas a motorhome won't go anywhere you couldn't drive the vehicle on which it is based, and because of the size and weight it is, in fact, even more limited.

I have used my Pajero to tow many a motorhome off a pitch that has become muddy after bad weather, whereas I could hook up my own caravan pitched next to it and drive off without any problem.

Motorhomes are much more expensive than towed caravans because you are also paying for the vehicle. If a motorhome suffers a mechanical failure or fails the MOT then the whole thing is off the road, whereas with a towed 'van you only need to access another vehicle with a tow bar and you are back on the road.

However, a motorhome is not usually as long as a vehicle/caravan combination, is more manoeuvrable, and can be parked in a more limited space. They are easier to maintain in a 'ready-to-go' condition so that if a Bug Out is required you can be underway very quickly. They are not subject to the same speed limits or licence requirements that a caravan is.

You can park either type at home or on a site with storage of course, but with a caravan you park it away and have your vehicle available for routine use whereas if you do the same with a motorhome you might need another car at home, so you are paying two lots of insurance, road tax, MOT, etc.

As with most things there are advantages and disadvantages to either and the choice comes down to which features are most important to you. There are magazines and Internet sites dedicated to either or both and lots of information available. If you haven't been caravanning, then before making a choice I suggest not only looking at various models of each at a dealers site, but hire each for a week or two, not just on a fixed site but also touring to get a real feel for which you prefer.

For sites you have quite a few choices. There are public sites or Caravan Club or Camping and Caravanning Club sites that offer full facilities including shower and toilet blocks, a shop, mains power, and much else for large numbers of caravans, motorhomes and tents.

Or there are CC/C&CC Certificate Sites/Locations which are small sites, often on a farm, that will only usually take 5 'vans, though they might have facilities/room for many more including tents. These sites usually offer far fewer extra facilities, some only having fresh water and a place to empty the chemical toilet, others also offering mains power, and a few have 1 or 2 toilets and showers. Or there are many independent farm sites with widely varying amounts of space and facilities and some of which are in very secluded places ideal as a BOL.

In an emergency you could also potentially go rogue and pull up anywhere you can find room to park but beware the opposition and prejudice you might face if you do so. Motorhomes are better for this type of camping because they are so self-contained, with onboard fresh and waste water facilities.

While on the subject of motorhomes: there is also a set of Preppers who appreciate the features of mobile homes but prefer a more discrete approach. These Preppers buy commercial vehicles of various types, from estate car sized vans to articulated lorries but the most popular is a high-top Ford Transit or Luton sized van. They decorate the outside to look like a trade vehicle that would contain few items of interest, or be positively unattractive, e.g. a pest controller, drain clearer, etc, and convert the inside with all the facilities of their choice. Their strategy is to Bug Out to wherever the situation dictates as a safe location and then hide in plain sight by parking among similar commercial vehicles. You could have parked next to one the last time you were at the supermarket and never known!

Boats

Like all other forms of BOL, boats have some great advantages but some disadvantages too.

Firstly, we must recognise that there are many different types, intended for many different forms of use and area of operation. To be of use as a BOL, rather than simply as transport, the boat must be large enough to offer accommodation and basic living facilities.

Without getting into vessels big enough to be classed as a ship, that still leaves you with: canal boats, river cruisers, sailing boats, coastal vessels, and ocean-going yachts. There are then a myriad of other choices such as: size, construction, method of propulsion, cost, equipment, etc, etc. If a boat becomes one of your choices then you will need to get into more specialised study than this book can provide. You can research online or using magazines or any of the thousands of books available.

All boats require appropriate skills for their safe handling and navigation, but obviously for those intended for off-shore travelling that is especially true. To operate a boat of 10m or under, (or 24m or under on suitable qualification) on inland or international waterways you will need at least an International Certificate of Competence (ICC). There are separate licences for sail or engine-powered boats.

In the UK, you can buy a boat up to 24m in length without any licence but to use it, gaining the skills by doing a course such as one offered by the Royal Yachting Association (RYA) and having those tested by getting the certificate is a highly recommended survival project if you intend to use any boat. You can then gradually increase your skills over time through study and practise. People die every year in non-emergency situations because they have taken to the water without the proper skills and knowledge.

Inland waterways, and even their waterside paths, are less well known and travelled by most of the population than normal footpaths, and on many stretches there is no public access to the banks at all. The rivers and canals themselves provide routes that are likely to be far less crowded or prone to blockages than any road.

Along some rivers there are quiet side channels that are hidden from open ground by banks of trees and protected by surrounding marshy conditions. Even canals have parts that aren't easy to approach. In these places you can indulge in discrete survival hunting and fishing of both land and water food sources, animal and vegetable.

Where a river is wide or opens into a lake/broad/loch, or if you head out to sea, then you can moor alongside either an inaccessible stretch of bank, shoreline or island, or out in deep water, so that you are difficult to approach by anyone other than in another boat.

If the situation deteriorates to the point that piracy becomes a problem, then you will obviously have to make provision for appropriate security just as land based Preppers do, but in the UK things would have to get pretty bad before that should be a concern.

In general, almost everything that I wrote about caravans and motorhomes also applies to this size of boat. You can be grid-free, mobile, and even a member of a like-minded and equipped group of Preppers. Inland waterways constrict you to the routes you can take but finding smaller unblocked roads means the same for caravanners, and if you go off-shore you have many options. Or you could find a suitable mooring and simply leave the boat there as a BOL rather than with any intention of using it as transport. You have choices.

We will look at boats again in the section on transport but for now consider, if you intend to use a boat as a BOL particularly for inland waterways or if you cross to Europe, you will need:

- A suitable boat

- Somewhere to keep or moor it as a BOL and/or when not in use

- A licence appropriate for your size and type of craft

- If the boat is powered, the Boat Safety Scheme (BSS) equivalent of an MOT for inland waterways is a requirement, and for sailing craft an RNLI Sea Safety Inspection is highly recommended.

- At least third-party insurance

Camp Sites

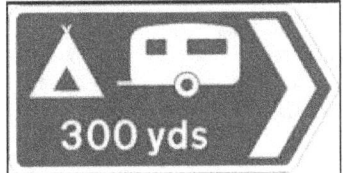
Basically, all the things I wrote above about caravan sites with regard to size, facilities and location, also apply to camping sites. However, the selection is even wider in this case, since some locations and pitches that would be difficult for a caravan to access are still suitable for tents.

If the situation that drove you out is relatively local, and you have a serviceable tent big enough and with sufficient other equipment for all occupants, and the weather conditions are not too severe, then a suitable camp site is a viable but much cheaper alternative to a hotel or even a B&B.

If the situation is more widespread, however, you could find the site quickly turning into an unofficial refugee camp, except with none of the supply or security systems. Then about the only difference between it and some of the camps you see on news footage is that the shelters, clothing kit and BMI of the refugees in the UK would be better, at least in the first few moths after the disaster.

The Wilderness

When many people overseas talk about Bugging Out their mind is automatically set on one of three scenarios: a pre-arranged communal retreat, a rural holiday cottage or similar, or in many cases, The Wilderness.

In some places, such as the USA, Canada, Australasia, Scandinavia, with large areas of sparsely inhabited country rich in natural resources, that might be a realistic option for those with the skills to survive there. Unfortunately in the UK it is not such a good idea. Here are things you should consider:

Most of our 'wilderness' areas are not wild at all. Every part of the UK actually belongs to someone, whether a private individual, company, or the state and many are worked or patrolled by employees who

know the area better than you ever can and who will be motivated to preserve the resources there for themselves and their employers, against intruders like you!

The parts that are less frequently visited are that way because they are bleak, barren, and inhospitable; of little use for even sheep farming, harbouring only deer or game birds. They offer little in the way of shelter or materials for building one, of reliable sources of animal or vegetable food, or of fuel but often an overabundance of water, much of it regularly coming in quantity from the sky as well as covering the ground.

The cause of your evacuation could be related to extreme weather, which might last far longer than you expect. Experienced well equipped people die in those areas every year due to accidents and exposure. Your chances of survival for any length of time after your rations and cooker fuel run out are narrow at best.

While I don't believe that most inhabitants of the UK would ever think of bugging out to the hills or forests, the few situations that might drive you to do so are likely to do the same for thousands of others with some outdoors experience.

All of them will have similar ideas, all competing for limited resources in small areas of countryside.

As much as you might visit these places now to practise in relative isolation, you are not doing so under conditions where there are people in competition with you who might see you as an even better source of supply than the local wildlife.

If things are so bad that you are bugging out to the wilds, then almost certainly there will have been a collapse of government and any rule of law. To survive in these circumstances, you will require not only the skills and knowledge of the competent hill walker and bushcrafter, but those of a soldier trained in combat survival.

You will need knowledge and experience of: moving unseen and without leaving tracks; making camouflaged shelters and gathering food and water unobserved; even going to the toilet while leaving no trace; practicing discipline in your use of ground and light and noise and scent; and much else. These things restrict every part of how you live and travel. A single mistake could prove fatal for you.

In addition, at least some of your over-confident competitors will not have your level of experience and will be starting fires, polluting water, scaring and wounding game, attracting predators, and generally making life more difficult and dangerous for you in many ways.

An individual or small group of similarly experienced people might be able to make it. It is possible. As a Combat Survival Instructor I have trained Service personnel and volunteers to do so while being hunted by enemy forces.

But they were fit, skilled and highly motivated young people who knew that if they could evade for long enough help was on its way. You would not have that relief.

And even then, with all the training and motivation, when it came to the real thing although some made it out some were captured, tortured and raped, and some were killed. Would you and your family be able to do better? What if your group includes elderly, sick or injured members, or children?

I'm not saying you should rule out heading for the woods/hills in all situations, but I have seen refugees fleeing across the plains of Africa and the mountains of northern Iraq and dying in droves in the attempt. Forget the Hollywood movies and think seriously about whether it is realistic for you and yours in the UK.

The fact is that for the majority of urban dwellers who don't know the countryside, its ways or its people, and even for most people who do but only in normal times, heading there after a disaster would be a fatal mistake.

Having given you those warnings, if you still believe that in the situation you face heading for the backwoods is your best option, where do you go?

To some extent it depends on where you live, of course. If you are on the south coast of England then the Scottish Highlands might be too far for you, so I won't make specific recommendations like that. However there might be places suited to you for close, medium and distant BOLs

If you get to know your local and potential BOL areas, as you should, you might find patches of woodland that are unused and rarely visited. Even a quick look at the general condition and any tracks that run through the area should give you a reasonable idea about that.

Short grass and recent tyre tracks are giveaways that it has been travelled through, but if the grass and brush at either side of the track is undisturbed, there are no noticeable parking spots, and the woodland floor is thick with bracken, brush and fallen branches, the track might just be a shortcut and the surroundings otherwise ignored.

In that case, especially if it is on private land not accessed by the public, this might be a possible BOL, if you use stealthy living practices.

If you choose to try more public ground, such as the national parks, then locate areas not visible from footpaths and far enough from them that any small sounds you make will go unheard. You also want somewhere more difficult to get to, maybe across a stream or around the other side of marshy ground or fallen trees. You should look for similar signs to those above to ensure it is/has been visited rarely if ever.

More likely to be travelled but still potentially viable and often with plenty of useful resources, are coastal stretches and near-offshore islands. Look carefully for the maximum height of tides before settling for any length of time and investigate for signs, and potential sources, of pollution before using shellfish or seaweeds. Land based plants are less likely to be affected.

Whatever the area, you want a pitch that is safe from dying trees or falling rocks, where you can make a dry, flat bed, that has plenty of materials for making a shelter, access to clean running water but not liable to flooding, near to sources of animal and plant food, and surrounded by undergrowth that will give you warning of anyone approaching ... and with a permanently dry, warm micro-climate would be nice. Dream on! There is more on covert backwoods living in the chapter on How to Survive.

There are plenty of options of where to go when bugging out. Some are more viable than others. Which are available depends on the situation. You should identify potential sites for as many as possible, in advance of them being needed.

Case Histories

In case you think a Bug Out to any of these locations is unlikely, let me give you a few examples of real situations that have arisen in just the past few years to people I know and have met:

In October 2012 I was chatting to someone we meet regularly on our main caravan site. He was currently living in his caravan because his ground floor flat in York had been flooded. There had been some warning in the area but even so the water rose so fast that in the late evening he had to grab a bag, stuff in what essentials he could think of, and escape on foot. Already the water was too deep to save his car.

Fortunately two of the items he snatched up on his way out were his wallet and phone, so he booked into a nearby hotel for the night. In fact he actually stayed for another two days until he could get home to salvage some of his possessions and move them to a self-storage facility. A garage towed his car away, drained and serviced it, and was able to get it running again, though he said he still needed to drive with the window open because of the smell. He then moved into his caravan as temporary accommodation.

The insurance company warned him that he could be living elsewhere for at least eight months after the water receded, while the flat was dried and repaired. He is still living in the caravan now. He told us that the main problems he struggled with since Bugging Out were due to the loss of all his paperwork, such as his insurance certificates for the flat and car. Other things he has lost, and missed since, are family photographs and all his documents for doing his end-of-year personal tax return, but he knows there are lots more that might be needed in future.

Also affected by flooding were some friends who live in

Hull. When they were flooded out they first went to the house of a family member, just a couple of streets away but uphill. They couldn't stay for long, there simply wasn't room, but it gave them somewhere for a few days rather than the hostel accommodation some of their neighbours had to accept.

Then the housing association arranged for static caravans, for them and others from their street, to be put in place on an industrial site not far away. Thankfully, these friends are Preppers and their grab bags ensured they were much less inconvenienced than our fellow caravanner.

Two years ago, while I was working in Oxford, I was shocked to find Bernie, a former soldier from my old unit, begging on the street. He was a young NCO when I was due out and served on after I left but had been discharged on medical grounds six years prior to this meeting. Since demob, he had suffered badly from PTSD, lost his job, his girlfriend, and eventually his house when it was repossessed. Unable to cope with the debt and stress, and with no reason to stay, he simply picked up his backpack and walked away. He had been living rough for eighteen months when I met him.

Initially, he told me, he headed for the local countryside and survived by using the skills he had been taught, but was eventually spotted and moved on by a gamekeeper, then thrown out of a barn by labourers on another farm, beaten up by yobs that found him asleep in a village sports pavilion, and suffered various other abuses. Eventually police took him from a hut beside a railway after he was discovered by people working on the line.

He then moved into town, slept rough, and on a desperately cold night broke into a canal boat. Next day people in the next boat reported him and he was arrested again. This time he spent the night in a cell, but at least got a shower and a couple of meals, then was given an official caution and released. Before they let him go, however, they brought in a social worker who gave him details of a local shelter and various other pieces of advice. He said the shelter was dire, that you even had to sleep with your boots on because otherwise somebody would steal them, but at least it was warm.

I bought us both a meal and sat while he told me his story. Then I gave him some money and later contacted our regimental association to see if they could help. I didn't see him again but when I called the association a couple of weeks later they told me that before they could contact Bernie, and just three days after I had been talking to him, he had been found dead in an alley in the city. His skull had been smashed in from behind and then he had been stabbed repeatedly. His battered old pack, coat and even his boots had been taken.

Bernie had been a good soldier, and was trained and skilled in rural and urban combat survival. Certainly he was physically, psychologically and emotionally damaged; a shadow of the man I had known. Even so, many of his military and later experiences were no worse than those you might suffer in a major disaster requiring a Bug Out to the wilds. It is his sufferings, and those I and other soldiers have experienced during survival situations, which lead to my caution that the common idea of Bugging Out could be far harder than most people expect.

When to Go

Ah, that's easy, Before IT happens!

What? You've not yet read the section on developing ESP? Hmm, in that case we'll have to look at other options!

In fact there are a couple of scenarios where you could Bug Out before an event. The first is where you move to your BOL as your usual residence and set up your life there. The second is when official sources, such as the Met Office or Environment Agency, provide you with advance warning.

In the latter case the best answer then becomes, 'As soon as possible.' That doesn't mean, take your time and do it when you are sure you have everything sorted, it means, WITH ALL DUE HASTE!

This is usually the biggest single mistake people make when faced with a disaster. Because of denial, confusion, and worry about what they are leaving behind, they delay too long, and in consequence experience far greater inconvenience, hassle and danger than they needed to. They are like people who risk death from burning or smoke inhalation rather than jumping from the first floor of a building on fire, because they are afraid they might break a leg.

The greatest advantage of being prepared for a Bug Out is that it can eliminate or substantially reduce that delay.

The idea in this situation is to get out before everybody else begins to do the same. After that the roads will soon become clogged with vehicles that have crashed, broken down, run out of fuel, or been abandoned by drivers panicking because they have been stuck for an hour in a traffic jam caused by one of the above.

You should certainly identify routes to your BOLs that avoid the main roads, including unconventional and normally illegal paths, but in some circumstances even getting to those can be made difficult by long lines of vehicles blocking your way to the exit you want.

This happened to me in the winter of 2010/2011. At the time I was working for a firm based to the north of Glasgow but south of the River Clyde. My route to and from the office was usually either via the M8/A80 through Glasgow or along back roads north of the river and over the Erskine Bridge.

One day, what had started as a relatively gentle snow fall became far heavier than had been predicted, across the whole of the Central Belt between Glasgow and Edinburgh. A series of closely-timed wet-snow related crashes on the motorways then brought traffic throughout the region to a standstill. The firm where I was working decided to send everyone home rather than them becoming stranded but for most the journey was to become a nightmare.

Having heard of the problems on the motorways I set off to cross the bridge and take the back roads home. This wasn't a concern to me because I was driving my Mitsubishi Pajero 4x4, fitted with winter tyres and with chains in the equipment box if they were needed. Before I reached the bridge I heard on the local radio channel that it was now closed because of the weather.

I turned around and headed out with the intention of crossing under the motorway and then taking a long way, heading east around the south side of the city before I could eventually turn north for home. Before long I found that not only was the motorway blocked so were all the on ramps and every standard road that led to those ramps. Vehicles were queuing back for miles from the start of the on ramps. Some of them were waiting to head up even though nothing on the motorway was moving, but they were also blocking the way for all the other vehicles behind them that didn't intend to use the motorway!

I then considered returning to the company and bugging in there, using the cache in my desk and the emergency kit from my car if needed, but I didn't know how long the situation would last and I wanted to be home to look after my family. I also knew that if I eventually did get completely stuck I had other options still available.

I turned again and eventually onto farm and forestry tracks until I was well clear of the motorway and the city before returning to the main roads. What was normally a 40 minute drive to get home took me seven and a half hours, but without the 4x4 I would undoubtedly have been stuck like many others who were stationary for up to 17 hours often with no resources and no support from any emergency services.

From the time of the first accident to complete gridlock was less than an hour.

I suffered a major delay and used lots of fuel but it was only because I had the 4x4 and had planned and driven a variety of alternative routes and tuned the radio to local travel news that I made it home so much faster than most. Many of them were delayed for longer than they should have been for all the reasons I mentioned above: vehicles ran out of fuel as the occupants kept the engine running to keep themselves warm; some were then abandoned as people tried to walk home; and the abandoned cars had to be recovered before the roads could be cleared.

All this happened so fast and simply because some articulated lorries skidded, jack-knifed and crashed at what happened to be critical points on the road system. That and the fact that the transport department was singularly ineffective in getting the situation sorted out.

Because this situation was so typical of stories from elsewhere when disasters strike, and could happen where YOU are, I urge you, prepare well and if you have to Bug Out do not delay for a minute longer than absolutely necessary.

If, for whatever reason, you are unavoidably delayed in setting off, then when do you go?

It depends on the reason you are bugging out and you will therefore have to re-evaluate. It could be that there is no choice but to evacuate ASAP and if you can't go by car then you will have to use some other form of transport, be it motorbike, bicycle, horse, on foot or whatever else you have available.

If the approaching threat would make being in the open potentially fatal, then you must consider whether you have a better chance if you batten down the hatches and Bug In. There are never any guarantees and you do what you have to do to give yourselves the best chance possible.

If, however, you are delayed when the threat is serious but not imminent, you might want to wait until the rush to escape has quietened down and you can at least move without being caught in panicking crowds. At this time you might be able to travel, possibly even drive, along footpaths, through private gardens and public parks, along the wrong side of the road and one way systems, and through other usually prohibited areas that would have been blocked during the mass evacuation.

Whatever the case, when a situation presents itself, be ready to move as soon as you can. In the meantime, use every resource you have to keep informed on the situation and how it is developing.

Speaking of which; I have a pair of hand-held CBs in the car that I sometimes use when travelling with people in another vehicle but we don't want to use mobile phones. I also kept one handy for use in an emergency, thinking I might be able to contact someone if I broke down or otherwise needed assistance.

On the day of the snow storm I tried every UK frequency several times, with both the built in antenna and a magmount roof antenna, trying to find out what was happening elsewhere on the roads, but never made contact with anyone or heard anyone else on air. The same has been true when I have tried since then. The sets work to one another at 5 miles so it isn't that. I guess CB is pretty much dead in the UK, or at least this part of Scotland and elsewhere I've tried it.

So: When do you go?

1) In advance of most dangers where possible by moving to live somewhere that those dangers will be minimised in the emergencies that are most likely and/or that will have worst impact.

2) At the earliest possible opportunity when you get warning of an imminent situation

3) As soon as it is safe if you have been unavoidably delayed.

How to Go

When you Bug Out, there are many different methods of travel you may use to get to your chosen BOL. Which of these are available to you depends mainly on the amount of time and effort you are willing to put into learning to use them.

For survival purposes you do not necessarily need to progress to the point where you gain the full licences to use all of these forms of transport. Essentially you have to be able to make it go, make it go where you want to go, and make it stop, preferably with both you and the transport in one piece.

However, the more skilled you become in the use of any vehicle, the greater the variety of conditions in which you will be able to use it effectively and the more sure you will be of getting to your destination. The more knowledgeable you become in its care and maintenance the longer it will continue to serve you.

To be useful, any form of transport must be able to move the group and their essentials for however far is required. Because of capacity you might need to use more than one example of the form. If so, safe movement will require you to adopt some special procedures, by travelling in convoy or formation for example. It will also require that you have sufficient fuel, tools and spares to keep you going for the whole journey despite possible hazards.

If you are travelling as a group then you should also have ways to communicate and to bring back into the fold anyone that becomes separated.

For best use of the transport you will have to consider the most efficient, effective distribution of loads, including people and various equipment and supplies, to ensure maximum safety and avoid the loss of all of any category of supplies if one of the vehicles is lost. Quite literally, don't put all your eggs in one basket, or fuel in one trailer.

And you should have plans in case you have to abandon

one of your methods of transport and move to another, such as leaving a van and moving onto bicycles, and perhaps eventually dumping the bikes and continuing on foot.

When you move you could, and might have to, move by land, water, and/or air. Moving by air is fastest and safest from most hazards but requires the most specialised skills. Travel on water is slowest under normal conditions but might be faster than by land in an emergency because of fewer obstacles and diversions. However travel by boat also requires some special skills, especially if you cross open water or use sails rather than an engine. Travel by land is the most familiar to the majority of people when they are in control of the transport but even here there are various options and to be able to take advantage of some would require you to invest in appropriate training. Each is covered in turn in this chapter.

Travel by land

In any emergency, most people trying to Bug Out from a mainland location will travel by land. If the situation is being caused by bad weather it might become the only viable option. Especially in bad weather you will probably want to travel by vehicle if possible and if so any transport you choose will become your Bug Out Vehicle (BOV).

What you must expect is that a mass of evacuees is going to create competition for resources, including fuel, road space, supplies of food, water, and other goods, and accommodation. Panic, fear, and anger are not going to improve the skills or judgement of any of the road users and will actively accelerate the crash rate and speed with which carriageways will become blocked.

As part of your preps you should have identified the less used roads and other byways that you could use to get to your various BOLs and the differing access routes to and from them. Depending on the capabilities of your transport, and of your drivers/riders, you might have included un-named roads, farm and forestry tracks, bridleways, towpaths, green lanes, open ground such as urban front gardens, pedestrian precincts and parkland, and open country where you could go fully off-road.

Often if you are driving on a minor road and find it blocked, you can get around the hold-up by going through a gate or dropping/cutting a fence and crossing a field or two. The same is true even from a major road if you have the tools to remove a section of crash barrier or a fence. Do watch out though for ditches, rocks or soft ground.

I can't emphasise enough how important a <u>realistic</u> appraisal of the capabilities of both transport and users is. I have seen more people stuck in remote places because of over-confidence in one or the other of those factors than I care to remember. There are an awful lot of 4x4 drivers out there who think they are set because they have the vehicle but who have never driven it off the main roads and many of them don't understand the controls or how to use them. High or low ratio – uh? Diff lock – say what?

Whatever forms of transport you plan/expect to have available, there are plenty of courses or clubs where you can learn to use your choices to an effective level and, for a Prepper, really no excuse for not doing so.

Car, Van, Motorhome, Bus or Truck

If you have a licence for a car, then in the main you can

 also drive a van or motorhome on that licence and technically there isn't a lot of difference.

There are some motorhomes that are so big they come into the same category as a bus or HGV and you need a different class of licence to drive them, but if something like that is your choice then presumably you are up for the extra costs and time involved in the upgrade.

Whichever type of vehicle you choose, your preference should be for a model that is reliable, fuel efficient, and big enough to take the people and load required. Off-road capability with four wheel drive and high ground clearance is a great bonus but comes with a cost in purchase price, maintenance and fuel consumption. Keep your BOV regularly serviced, well maintained, and with the tank never less than three quarters full.

Equip the vehicle with a Car Kit and if possible store your short-term/local area pack on-board as well (see the chapter 'What to Take' for what should be in these kits). Cover the load and scatter ordinary items such as coats and bedding on top before bugging out, to hide your good stuff.

Type of fuel is your choice but have at least a tank full of spare fuel stored in cans and add a fuel preservative to extend the storage life. Petrol without preservative can break down within six months to the point where it will not run your car, though you will have fewer problems if it is mixed with fresh fuel. Diesel lasts longer but the preservative will help to prevent water contamination and extend the useful life even further.

Consider that although diesel is more expensive it is safer to store and beyond ordinary filling stations there are more sources for it than there are petrol, particularly outside urban areas. Diesel is often stored in bulk on farms, marinas, and railway depots.

Most diesel engines will run on domestic heating fuel, aviation fuel, or cooking oil. In the long term you could grow suitable crops that will provide the oil so that you could make your own fuel.

Alternatively, consider a Propane conversion. Propane stores without deterioration for extremely long periods and is available in many rural areas, caravan sites and dealers, and council roads and works depots.

If you have space in the garage, you might want to have a towing ball and single electrics fitted to your vehicle and then buy a trailer, which you can keep loaded ready for even a long distance Bug Out. To avoid temptation to thieves both in storage and on the move get one with a lockable hard top, or at least use a chain and padlock to securely lash down a heavy duty cover.

Keep the trailer serviced, leave the handbrake off and chock the wheels if necessary. Have a spare wheel for the trailer. Check all tyre pressures regularly. If the trailer is really not often going to move, put it up on axel stands to relieve pressure on the tyres and extend their life. Leave a trolley jack under the trailer so that you can quickly dismount it if you have to Bug Out at short notice.

Learn to load and tow a trailer safely. Courses are available but as basics: distribute the load evenly; too much weight at the front makes it difficult to hitch and unhitch, too much at the back can cause the trailer to 'fishtail' dangerously as you drive. Be especially careful when loading heavy items, such as a generator or cans of fuel or water; the best place for them is in the centre, over the wheels.

Try to drive slowly and smoothly and remember to allow for the length of the trailer when overtaking and cornering. When reversing a trailer, have someone guide you and be aware that to get the trailer to go left you turn the steering wheel to the right and vice versa. Towing mirrors can be helpful and for some trailers are required.

Fit a good lock to your garage door; most of the ones fitted in a central handle are next to useless. If you have a mechanical opener, ensure it can be overridden if the power supply is off.

You probably don't want to buy a bus or lorry but if you learn to drive them then in an emergency you might be able to take possession of one. They are less manoeuvrable than smaller vehicles and use more fuel but they have the advantages of great storage capacity and the bulk and weight to push smaller vehicles out of the way, if needed. Allow for the length and width, and heavy steering, when turning or reversing.

There is much more information on security while travelling in the chapter on 'How to Survive'.

Motorbikes

Lightweight motorcycles can be very useful bug-out vehicles for various situations and even heavier bikes can get through gaps in traffic or other obstructions and along narrow tracks where a 4 wheel vehicle can't go.

A light bike won't have the power that a big one will, or its comfort for long distance cruising, but its manoeuvrability, responsive handling, and fuel efficiency are big pluses. This makes something like a 125cc road or trail bike a tempting choice for an urban escape vehicle and for an individual Prepper, or a couple with a bike each, this could be a highly practical option.

The load carrying capacity is severely limited compared to a car; in fact you are pretty much confined to a couple of panniers and a backpack, but even then you can take more than you would want to carry if travelling on foot or a bicycle. However, don't forget that you will need to give some of that load weight to tools and possibly to spare fuel.

Small motorcycles are also relatively easy to hide, so if you are heading for a rural BOL you should be able to get close to your chosen site, conceal the bike and then finish the journey on foot, to where you might have caches available.

Any rider is unavoidably more vulnerable to attack and

environmental conditions than someone surrounded by metal, but the acceleration and quick handling can enable you to avoid or escape from situations that would trap a 4 wheel vehicle.

As part of a larger group, light motorcycles also serve well as mounts for scouts and outriders and in this case most of their kit can be carried in the cars.

As a real life example of a similar use: A while ago I corresponded online with a young man in Indonesia. He was a fisherman and therefore lived on the coast. Dur had already once before narrowly escaped with his life when the area was hit by a Tsunami. He didn't get away unscathed however; he lost a leg due to it becoming crushed by debris, and all the rest of his family were killed.

Knowing that he was now slower and less able if his home village was hit again, Dur invested in a moped and became familiar with all the routes he might use, and landmarks by which he could navigate, to higher ground. When the next warning came, he took to the bike, picked up his girlfriend from her work and headed out. Weaving around the fleeing pedestrians and cars stuck in traffic, he made it to safety in time for them to be able to watch as the wave hit, destroying most of the village.

Dur might not have been a Prepper as we think of it. He had no store room full of canned goods or other gear. But he recognised a threat and a potential problem; decided what was needed to overcome them and survive, and did what he had to do. That makes him a Prepper to me!

If it suits your family or group circumstances, a lightweight motorcycle is worth of serious consideration as a BOV.

Bicycle

If you want a no-fuel, lightweight, licence-less, faster-than-walking mode of transport then it has to be a bicycle.

As advantages: it will go anywhere a lightweight motorcycle will and more, if not as quickly; where you can't ride you can wheel or even carry it; maintenance is relatively easy; it's quiet; no fuel needed for the bike – though more is for the rider than on powered transport; still comparatively cheap to buy and run; it is a less obvious and desirable target than a motorbike.

Disadvantages: it takes physical effort to use, which becomes more difficult as high calorie food becomes scarcer; until you are used to it certain sensitive areas of your body will get sore (!); you are as vulnerable as on a motorcycle but you don't have as much speed with which to escape; because of physical effort needed, carrying capacity is even less.

If you are fit and cycle regularly so that you develop and maintain the right muscles for cycling, however, this certainly has some advantages over walking. There is a wide variety of models available with prices ranging from very affordable to 'HOW MUCH?' but I was pleasantly surprised when researching this section that at the budget end prices are not bad at all.

There are still racing and 'road' bikes available, along now with mountain bikes, but there is also a breed called the Hybrid that is a cross between a road and a mountain bike that might fill the Prepper niche very nicely. That is especially true if for you a bicycle is for general use and as a backup for bugging out, rather than as primary transport.

There are also the folding bikes, which perhaps have uses for bugging in but most of which I suggest are too slow and demand too much energy output to be realistic for more than local use. There are, though, some with 18 or 20 inch wheels and even folding mountain bikes with up to 18 gears. These might suit you better as fall-back transport if carried on/in a motor vehicle, though they do fall in the middle of the price spectrum.

Preppers who are not so fit or agile might want to consider one of the bicycles with an electric motor added. That feature can be useful if kept in reserve for when really needed but at the cost of extra weight and the requirement to carry some way of recharging the battery. Because of the limited range (30-80Km) with power and the additional weight I would, again, only recommend these for local Bug Outs or use close to home. They are not cheap either; £800-2000 seems to be the normal price range.

You can also offset the limited carrying capacity of a bicycle by adding a trailer. Specific models are made for cargo and others for small children or pets. Some of those for babies and toddlers also work as a pushchair and/or carrycot. They do restrict your manoeuvrability somewhat but most do not significantly widen the outfit.

If a bike is for you, don't forget to add a good tool kit and selection of spares, plus appropriate protective clothing.

Horses and carts

I must admit, I don't really get on with horses. It's not that I don't like them, despite having had them kick me, bite me, and tread on my foot, which isn't good from a 17hands high Shire weighing about 'bloody heavy!'

Fortunately the ground was soft and I was wearing safety boots otherwise I'd probably need a shoe twice as wide on that foot as the other.

No, I like them OK and I learned the basics of how to look after them and to ride well enough not to fall off,  most of the time, going cross country but they wouldn't be my first choice as transport.

That said, I recognise their advantages and I know there

are lots of people out there who would disagree with my reservations about the equine species. They have, after all, been the most common form of transport internationally for centuries.

Certainly they are an option you should not ignore and which you should learn to use.

After an emergency of global proportions they might soon become the most viable choice and even on a more local scale there are enough around that it doesn't make sense not to be able to take advantage of their capabilities.

Differing breeds could be used for either riding or pulling a cart during a Bug Out. Even without a cart a spare horse can carry a lot of luggage. They require no artificial fuel and can usually get by on natural grazing except in extremely sparse conditions but if working they do benefit from food supplements, such as oats. They can cross even worse ground than a scramble bike and are capable of sustained speed.

You do need skills to ride or drive them and lessons are not cheap but they really are essential for safety of yourself and the horse, not to mention just getting it to go where you want it to.

You must also learn about proper fitting and maintenance of harness and other accoutrements and about general care. And you need to build and harden the various muscles and fleshy areas that are new to this type of activity. Expect to suffer for a while!

There are also many forms of cart, suited to differing sizes and breeds of horse and for differing purposes. These range from light open-top one or two person buggies, to covered carriages and flatbed farm carts. Each of these has its own form of harness and steering mechanisms for one or more horses.

Horses and their associated forms of transport offer a tremendous resource and it is a subject on which I can offer only the most basic of advice and opinion, but the information is out there and if you see this as a subject of particular relevance and benefit to you then by all means go for it.

And then, please, just watch for me beside my fuel-less trail bike thumbing for a ride, and don't be surprised if I step wide of the beast while climbing on board!

On Foot

Well now we are getting down to the basics; boots on the ground! For many people bugging out this will be how they start and for many more how they end up after abandoning their transport for one reason or another.

I would guess that a fair proportion of readers of this book have at least a passing familiarity with hiking and backpacking but for some it will have been a while ago and others of you will never have walked more than a few miles at most and then not with a pack full of the essentials for living away from home.

I say a 'pack', but if you watch news reports of any evacuation you will see personal possessions being moved in suitcases, shopping bags, pillow cases, shopping trolleys, prams, wheelbarrows, and just about any other means of storage and transport you can think of.

I have a small luggage trolley with an extending handle. It is designed for suitcases that don't have the built-in wheels many now feature. Although it functioned as it was, the small wheels did not work well over any ground rougher than a normal pavement, so I fitted a modified axel and a set of child's bicycle wheels. With a standard rucksack strapped on, it has proved to be a workable alternative over many hikes and camping trips for a family member with spinal problems that make backpacking extremely painful.

The next chapter in this book is called, 'What to Take'. In the lists that chapter contains, there are some items that are essentials in almost any Bug Out situation and many others that are options. Some might not be relevant if you are heading for an official shelter, hotel, or friend's house but vital if you intend to, or eventually have to, camp out.

More than with any other method of transport, it is so important if any part of your Bug Out plan includes travelling on foot, that you pack all items you expect to Bug Out with, into the containers you intend to use, dress in the clothes you have planned to wear, and then get out and walk with them for at least an hour.

A daytrip is better. Only in this way will you get any idea of the weight and discomfort levels and whether you are going to be able to cope. If not, either change the plan or look at ways to lighten the load or different ways to move it.

After you have done the walk, either measure the distance you covered as accurately as you can on a map, or if you walked on pavements zero the trip meter on your car then drive the route alongside it and note the distance. This will give you a proper measure of the miles covered in that first hour or day.

Forget about 'walking speed' being 5 mph; in fact that is a brisk marching pace for trained troops and for most people it would be a trot. Walking speed varies according to: the type of ground being walked on e.g. pavement, flat grass, heather hillside; the slope being walked up or down; the fitness of the walker and the load they are carrying. Weather and the clothing you are wearing can also affect your pace.

A regular walker might average 3mph and walk for 7 or 8 hours, a newbie with a load perhaps 2mph over 6 hours actual walking time, not including halts or pauses, though having a bush fire or flesh eating zombies close behind might push your pace and endurance somewhat. If you have children, elderly or infirm with you, your pace and total distance covered will inevitably be considerably reduced.

Unless you are a seasoned hiker, the distance you cover each hour will decrease in proportion to the number of hours you have walked. The further you go the slower you will be and the more and longer rests you will need each hour, until eventually you just have to stop.

Remember too that you will need to regularly drink water, and to find sources to refill your water supply as you go, and to eat either at some stops or as you walk.

Blisters on your feet and sores rubbed elsewhere by bag straps or ill fitting clothing will gradually decrease your tolerance and increase your body's demand to halt. This will be worse on the second day and almost intolerable on the third. Then, if you have been treating your wounds effectively and getting decent rest before walking again, it gradually gets better.

Going off this idea yet? That isn't my aim, I promise you. The fact is that if you are going to live there might be no alternative for you and your family than to lace on your boots, pick up your bags and walk away from your home. I just don't want anyone to think that doing so is going to be painless.

The more you understand of the reality, the less shock it will be and the less damage it will do to your morale. If you have to go, and you do so knowing it isn't easy for anyone, not just you, but that you simply have to get on and do it, and that you can if you have the determination, you are more likely to survive.

Travel by water:

In the course of my work I have spent time on islands or mainland Europe and had to include plans to travel by air or water as the first part of my Bug Out from where I was in order to return home to mainland Britain.

At other times I have planned to use a boat to get from point to point down a river or as the quickest way from one side of a lake to the other or as a backup to cross a waterway if my Bug Out by road or on foot was blocked by collapsed bridges.

Elsewhere it was one means of evacuation from a war zone to a safer place from which normal travel could be made. For many people recently it has been their means of bugging out, or being rescued, from a flooded home, though a word of warning: navigation and avoidance of obstacles below the surface can be much more difficult and hazardous when the normal waterways boundaries and their features are hidden by the wide and murky waters of flooding. Your journey might face similar challenges.

Generally, travel in troubled times is quieter, less hindered, and safer by water than by road, though the journey is often longer and slower. For example, if the country was in turmoil, with people fleeing south from Scotland, it would be a far easier journey to sail from any part of the Scottish coast to a port in England than it would to travel by one of the few roads and through bottlenecks in the central belt.

Boats might become crowded but they could hardly get as bad as those over-loaded death traps from parts of Asia or North Africa when refugees try to use a similar way to escape from those places.

Even for shorter journeys it is a useful option. Imagine trying to evacuate from central London through streets full of panicking residents and visitors, half not really knowing where they were going, and then think about the alternative of sailing down the Thames and then north to Norfolk or beyond. If the weather was kind, the latter would be pleasure trip by comparison.

Then again, some secure and sheltered Bug Out locations are only reasonably accessible by use of a boat. I know of several unused, tree-and-grass-shrouded islands in rivers, lochs, and close offshore, and quite a few inlets surrounded by steep cliffs, which fall into that category.

So, sometimes travel by water would be the preferred method and sometimes your only choice for at least a part of the journey. Either way, the ability to competently use various types of water craft is a valuable skill, though one that does sometimes require specialised training, and almost always demands specialised equipment, in order to ensure a safe trip.

Canoe/Kayak/Rowing or motor boat inc. inflatable/Sailing dinghy

These smaller boats are good choices for most inland waterways, though some variants will also serve for coastal use. Various types are used for fishing and recreational sailing including touring and waterside camping, and for casual or serious competition.

The open boats tend to have room for more people or cargo than the Kayak, but the Kayak has better protection and can tackle rougher water.

A motor gives you the advantage of not using energy while travelling but the others benefit from not needing any fuel. A sailing dinghy requires dexterity and skill and does need wind but doesn't always place constant demands on your endurance, though fast movement and handling are sometimes required. These craft do not require any special licences but some areas of water do impose restrictions and demand users to hold a permit. Remember too that some lakes and lochs are on private property and the same laws of trespass apply as on the surrounding land.

The basic skills to use the paddle powered boats are almost instinctive and develop quickly with practise but even a couple of sessions with an instructor makes a huge difference to your efficiency e.g. using a sweep stroke to turn instead of a back paddle, and slightly rougher conditions can make proper training essential. When venturing onto water you should always wear appropriate protective clothing and inflation aids, of course, but professional training is only sensible if you plan to enter what is, for most people, a foreign environment.

If your aim in using a boat is to aid you in survival, it is hardly logical to put yourself at risk by doing so without sufficient competence or gear! Find a club that operates under the regulations of the appropriate body e.g. royal Yachting Association (RYA) or British Canoe Union (BCU) and take advantage of the knowledge available there.

In addition to the basic equipment for the craft, you should have either waterproof bags or dedicated containers for your other possessions. Water invariably gets into any boat and there is always the chance of capsize so secure the bags to the boat to avoid losing them. This also gives the side benefit of reducing the amount of water a swamped boat can hold, making bailing out faster. As with any sport or activity there is lots of other specialised kit available but if you are only using the craft as transport you won't need most of it.

Canal boat/Motor cruiser

I mentioned these before in the chapter 'Where to Go' since they can be both transport and accommodation. In some cases they might be at a permanent mooring and you will need one of the smaller boats to get to them. Alternatively you might plan to use them as transport to a pre-selected secluded and well resourced spot and then tie up there as your BOL. Most run on diesel and some are exceptionally fuel-efficient, but many canals were built with a towpath so with a good horse you might be able to go back to using that if fuel becomes unavailable. With a suitable harness you could even pull a light narrow boat yourself

Motor cruisers operate on rivers, lakes and Broads as well

as canals. Size of both cruisers and canal boats varies widely. Smaller ones are easier to handle, larger ones have more accommodation and cargo space. You need training to handle either, including knowledge of navigating on waterways and how to operate locks on canals, but boating offers a very pleasant holiday activity and the learning is a pleasant experience.

Yacht/Trawler/etc

If you intend to go out further than inshore, or operate in rougher weather and waters, then you need a bigger boat, some serious skills, and a competent crew. With these, your Bug Out options are vastly enhanced but the costs and time involved to develop them are much greater. If this is something you consider seriously as a way forward, be prepared for what might become a lifetime of commitment.

Jet ski/Amphibious car/paddle boat

OK, it sounds like a bit of a joke but I thought I'd include them for the sake of completeness.

An amphibious vehicle would actually be a very useful BOV but they are rare and expensive. If you have one, you already know what you can do with it; if you haven't got one, don't worry about it!

One or two of the lochs and lakes with islands that I mentioned, do have firms around them that hire out paddleboats to the tourists. The enclosed waters are invariably calm, though deep enough to ensure only a boat or strong swimmer could reach the islands. Although these havens are privately owned, and peppered with notices declaring them off-limits, most are not inhabited and are rarely visited, so you do inevitably see young couples ignoring that and using the landing spots that are easily available, to take advantage of the privacy they offer . In less normal times you might want to do the same though with different intentions but be aware that might also be exactly the reason some of the people who own them do so! In past times, some of these islands were used by locals to protect their stock from theft by competing clans or border reivers.

Travel by air:

Light aircraft/Helicopter

Yes, I am serious. Developing the skills to fly a light aircraft or helicopter is not beyond the ability of most people, though the cost might be. To gain a fixed wing Private Pilot Licence (PPL) will, on average, take between 45 and 60 hours flying time and you have to take both a practical test and 8 written tests. Cost will typically be £8-10,000. Some of that will carry over to flying a rotary wing (helicopter) but expect more time. Cost will be £10-15,000.

As I said earlier you don't have to go all the way to achieve and maintain a PPL for each class but it is still going to cost you. Learning to fly a helicopter is more difficult but it offers the typical rotary advantages of manoeuvrability and a wider choice of landing places. You can learn some things from a PC based flight simulator but it is NOT the same as a commercial flight simulator and certainly not the same as the real thing.

The major returns on your investment would be speed of travel and safety while in the air. Accidents do happen but they tend to make the headlines, while car crashes are usually relegated to the local papers, because air crashes are so rare by comparison. Small fixed or rotary wing aircraft have fairly limited cargo capacity but you could certainly carry a BOB for each person and some extra supplies and kit.

Flying isn't for everyone but if you do have the chance to learn it is a considerable extra skill set for your Prepper CV.

To summarise: there are many forms of travel available, by land, water or air. Which you can access and use depends mainly on what skills you are willing and able to develop. Courses are available. The more options of which you can take advantage the better your chances of survival.

What to take

Some survival gurus recommend carrying a tobacco tin sized survival kit on a daily basis, with the contents adapted to the area in which you are living or working. However, I find that after a while many people come to regard them as an inconvenience and often leave them behind, or at best drop them into a bag – which isn't always with them - rather than their pocket. For most of us it's more convenient to spread the important items around our clothing or put them in something, like a wallet or purse, which will always be taken. They are then more likely to be there when we need them.

Some of these items almost everyone would carry every day. Preppers add a couple of things to the list and when they get home will leave it all in the pockets of a jacket by the exit, or drop it into a small bag ready to grab-and-go.

Some extra items are particularly recommended by regular travellers on the underground or who commute by train. They have found them useful when stuck between stations for a prolonged period.

These then form the basics of

Every Day Carry (EDC):

Money inc. coins for machines
Credit/debit card
Plastic driving licence (photo ID if required)
Mobile phone- there are lots of potentially useful apps available
Keys – house, car, local BOL, etc.
Tissues
Torch – either pen type or on your key ring
Spectacles
Personal medicines e.g. aspirin, asthma inhaler, insulin

Pen or pencil

A small notepad, or sheets of waterproof paper in wallet/purse

Disposable lighter

Wrist watch – their use is declining as people rely more on the mobile phone, but a watch will keep running long after a phone battery has died.

Pocket knife with: non-locking blade, scissors, wood saw, metal saw/file, pliers, tin opener, screw drivers, corkscrew, toothpick, tweezers. This is UK legal for EDC but will be banned from some places such as aircraft, night clubs, etc. Some people prefer a model with fewer – or more, or different - tools.

Condom or zip lock poly bag – in wallet/purse?

Water purifying tablets – in wallet/purse?

Mini pry bar – on key ring

Whistle – on a lanyard or key ring

Nylon cord – could have replaced shoe laces or draw cords in a coat or be worn as a bracelet

Ferrocium rod - on your key ring

An SD card or small USB drive containing scans of important documents, family photographs, and reference texts

If away from home add:

Street/area map of wherever you are

Miniature compass

If you are carrying a briefcase or shoulder bag you might add more of some EDC items e.g. tissues, plus:

Bottle of water

Snack foods

Strong leather gloves

Compact rain jacket or disposable poncho with hood

Warm hat

Spare socks and underwear

Large bandana or handkerchief

First aid pouch - plasters, wound dressing, safety pins, surgical tape, pain killers, antihistamine, antiseptic wipes/cream, superglue, etc
Antiseptic hand wash
Baby wipes
Tampons
Dental floss
Small radio
Sewing kit
Spare spectacles or a folding magnifying glass if required
Emergency charger for mobile phone
Spare batteries
Folding shopping bag
Book
Candles – birthday cake type or tea/nightlight
Spoon or Spork
Smoke/dust/bio masks
Surgical gloves
Disposable shoe covers

Some Preppers will add much more, such as a metal mug, wire, tape, etc, but few of the objects above would raise any eyebrows and, despite it seeming a long list, if they are chosen with care examples are available that work well but are compact and light weight and therefore much more likely to become routine parts of your EDC.

Car Kit

A car emergency kit can serve many purposes. You will find it a great comfort, as I have, if you break down or become stuck due to motorway hold-ups, bad weather, or many other factors.

It can save you money you might otherwise have spent booking into a hotel or eating at a motorway café, take care of your bodily needs, and keep you warm and amused while others shiver and argue with their fellow passengers.

It can serve as a cache for your workplace or local area, and in a Bug Out situation will give you tools to get you out of a traffic jam.

The car kit is another part of your overall Bug Out equipment, but more likely to be used than anything other than your EDC. It extends the EDC and although you are unlikely to be in the car without your everyday items it does duplicate some to extend the duration of use or act as spares for passengers who don't have them.

The list also includes special items for babies and pets, which might or might not be applicable for you, but they're there in case you do need them.

Some of the contents might be used frequently, in which case you will want to keep them close to hand around the driver's area, others can usually stay in a bag or box in the boot, but if you know you are heading out into bad weather it would make sense to bring them into the body of the car, so that you avoid having to get cold and wet fetching them if you do get stuck.

Warmth:

Blankets (2 minimum)
Thick socks
Gloves
Hat
Emergency ponchos (2)

Food and drink:

Water 5L+
Filter

Water purification tablets
Gas stove + extra cartridge
Matches or disposable lighter
Mess tins
KFS
Mugs
Food – packets or tins, not dehydrated, for easy/no prep with limited water supplies. Choose things that won't freeze in winter or melt in summer.
Drinks

Comfort:

Toilet paper
Baby wipes
Cling film
Zip lock bags
Male/female pee bottle
Tissues
Hand cleanser

Lighting:

Wind-up head torch
12v charged torch

Navigation and signalling etc:

Car - phone charger
CB
Maps – local and national
Satnav
Reading glasses

Notebook
Pen and pencil (with eraser)
Glow sticks
Compass
Whistle

First Aid Kit:

Sterile gloves and masks
Artificial respiration aid
Hand cleanser gel
Wound dressings
Burn dressings
Triangular bandages
Surgical scissors
Adhesive dressings
Steri wipes
Germolene
Antihistamine
Insect repellent
Tape
Painkillers
Pro-plus
Prescription meds
Space blankets

Tools and Miscellaneous:

This list does not include normal car tools such as spanners or screwdrivers that should always be carried, but if there are special types of those items they will be mentioned.

Spanners and socket set – with heads that will fit the bolts on roadside crash barriers. So that you can remove a

section if that gives you a chance to get off a blocked road.
Pry bar
Hatchet – with the saw, for cutting away parts of a fallen tree so you can pass rather than making a long detour or through a wooden fence so you can get onto farm/forestry tracks or go cross country to a clear road
Folding saw
Bolt croppers – for cutting fence wire and padlocks
Hacksaw – for stronger padlocks (cutting the hasp or staple is often easier)
Duct tape and insulating tape – for general repairs
Spare fuel
Inverter - power tools, running/recharging the laptop, etc
Sunglasses - good in snow conditions as well as bright sunlight
AA/RAC/Etc membership card
Folding shovel – winter kit
Tyre snow socks or chains – winter kit
Grip mats – winter kit
Bag of salt/grit mix – winter kit

The following items will not be relevant for everyone. I have included shelter and fire making kit for an Event that catches you away from home and any of your chosen BOLs or any other better choice and so requires you to make a temporary camp. Your personal circumstances may make that unlikely for you, if so ignore these items. Similarly the Baby and Pet kits might not be applicable to you.

Shelter:

Bivvy sheets
Ground sheet
Parachute cord

Fire Making:

Matches
Lighter
Flint and striker
Tampons
Tea lights

Baby Bag/Kit:

Nappies
Wipes
Spare clothes
Bottle and/or bowl & spoon
Food
Blanket
Cuddly toy
Dummy (Pacifier) if used
Medicines if required
Push chair/carrier

Dog Kit:

Collar and extending lead
Poo bags
Food and Water bowls
Food and treats
Water
Towel

Bug Out Bags

Now we are getting to the part where many books similar to this one start, and where quite a few end too!

These kits don't assume that you will have your car kit available but if you do it will be a bonus. The kits do assume you will have the on-the-body items of your EDC as those should be at least as easily accessible as the bigger kits are as you run from the house!

These kits are modular in nature. First there is an **Essential Documents kit**, which contains paper copies of all the things that the name implies. There should be electronic copies of these on the SD card/USB drive that is part of your EDC but some authorities demand the originals and waiting for a new copy of those from the originators could impose an inconvenient wait.

In many cases you don't need every piece of paper relating to these matters. An insurance certificate or recent pay statement might be enough for most purposes relating to those things rather than all the policy and employment paperwork, for example. However, you should have something to prove any claim you might make. This whole pack might fit into a couple of plastic document wallets. Ours is in a leather document folder placed inconspicuously but ready to grab on our way out.

Then there is a **short-term or local area kit**. Most of the contents of this are the sort of thing you would put into a weekend bag for a stay at a hotel, caravan, or even with a friend e.g. a full set of clothes, toiletries, etc but it is also what you will need if you have to run from a house on fire in the middle of the night, wearing nothing but a nervous smile.

I keep this kit in the car, so we do not duplicate things like the dog kit that is part of the car set up, but your circumstances might differ. Our kit is in a large holdall type bag with built-in wheels and extending handle but a suitcase, backpack, or several smaller bags would serve the purpose as well.

Finally there is the **Long-term or wide area kit**. This is what most people would think of as a **Bug Out Bag (BOB).** In fact it's a bag for each person. These are totally independent from the other kits, and packed in backpacks. Kids should have their own packs, scaled according to their age and ability to carry, or drag if placed on a trolley. For younger children those won't hold much but every ounce you haven't had to carry will be welcome come the end of a long day. Some items will serve for the whole group and these should be shared among the loads of those who can carry them.

When making your plans with these bags you must be realistic. There is no point putting together a backpack full of all the kit a soldier would use in the field if you have trouble walking to the bus stop or carrying a bag of shopping. If you can improve your fitness then do. If not, make your arrangements to match your capabilities.

The BOB includes items that do duplicate things in the car kit, but the concept is that you might have to grab the BOB and quite literally run for your life rather than taking the car, or if you have bugged out in the car you might have to abandon it at short notice and have a bag that you can grab and go without searching for things in the car kit to transfer to another bag.

Initially, you might not want, or be able to afford, two lots of kit. If that is the case then I suggest you store the BOB in the car if you have one and grab it from there if you have to leave on foot, rather than storing some things in the car and others in a bag elsewhere. In the end though, it is your decision as to what works best for you.

The Essential Documents Kit

You should include:

Personal identification documents – Passports, birth certificates, driver/pilots/sailing licences, national insurance details, national health card, firearms and shotgun certificates, etc

Family documents – marriage certificates, divorce papers, adoption papers, family tree, contact details for family members, photographs
Legal essentials – wills, powers of attorney, pre-nuptial agreements, house deeds, rental agreements, contact details for legal representatives, organ donor cards, patents, etc

Insurance policies – Home, life, medical policies, etc

Financial – bank account books/details, spare credit/debit card, savings books and policies, share certificates, receipts for expensive items (for use in insurance claims), electronic copy of business accounts, cash including notes and small change for phones and vending machines etc, (remember that in many emergencies electric power might be out and cash machines or card readers in shops not working, so some cash is an essential) some emergency trade/payment items e.g. gold or silver coins.

Professional – copy of your CV, current employer details, latest pay statement, tax documents e.g. in the UK, P60 and P45, electronic copy of any manuscripts or other documents you have written, drawings you have made, educational and professional qualification diplomas, certificates and association membership records

Vehicle – registration document, MOT certificate (roadworthiness document), vehicle insurance certificate, tracker agreement and code, for any road vehicles, boats, aircraft, etc, that you own.

Medical – medical records, prescription details, spectacle prescription, medical insurance details/policy,

Household – contact details for your utility providers inc. electricity, gas, water, TV, Internet, telephone, home care, etc – so you can call and tell them your supply/agreement is no-longer valid. Records of all your internet log-on/user names, passwords, etc.

Emergency contacts – Fire, ambulance, police, local numbers, doctor, vet, family and friends, employers, insurance companies, banks, - you will have some of these on other paperwork but a single document with all the contact details and relevant references will save you time and frustration when you could surely do without it.

House and car keys – a spare set

Short-term/local disaster kit

1 full set of clothes for each person in the group, inc:
2 sets underwear
2 pair socks
1 pair shoes/trainers/boots
1 pair trousers
1 Belt
1 T shirt
1 flannel shirt or similar
1 sweater or fleece
1 waterproof jacket
1 warm hat
1 pair gloves
1 scarf or bandanna

Wash kit, inc:
Liquid soap
Shampoo
Toothbrush per person
Toothpaste
Dental floss
Razor(s)
Hairbrush
Comb
Toilet roll per person
Baby wipes
Tampons or pads
Metal mirror
Towel per person
Flannel per person

Personal medicines pack:
Prescription medicines for each person who needs them, plus a copy of the repeat prescription form.
Spectacles in current strength/prescription for each user
Hearing aid and batteries – as required

First Aid Kit, inc:
Adhesive dressings
Wound dressings
Burn dressings
Antiseptic wipes
Antiseptic cream
Antihistamine cream
Ibuprofen gel
Pain killers e.g. aspirin, codeine, paracetamol, or stronger if appropriate and available
Antihistamine tablets
Antacids
Diarrhoea relief pills
Travel calm - as required

Oral thermometer
Tweezers
Scissors
Safety pins
Antibiotic hand gel
Surgical gloves
Surgical masks

Other items:
Sewing kit
PAYG mobile phone
Personal management radios – ideally 1 per person old enough to use it (mobile phone net could be down)
Torch per person
Spare batteries
Wind-up/solar radio (for news, etc)
Whistle per person
Pocket knife or multi-tool per responsible person
Local area maps and road map
Compass
Notebook
Pencils and pens
Books or games as required
Bottle of water per person
Snack foods

Baby Kit

Nappies
Wipes
Spare clothes
Bottle and/or bowl & spoon
Food
Blanket
Cuddly toy

Dummy (Pacifier) if used
Medicines if required
Push chair/carrier

Dog kit
Poo bags
Food and Water bowls
Food and treats
Water
Towel

Long term/wide area affected kit (BOBs)

Much of this kit should only be required if your plans to reach a BOL go wrong or if you need it while moving to that BOL. Once there you should be in better accommodation and with better facilities than any BOB can provide. Nevertheless, a well selected bag of equipment and supplies is a useful part of the Bug Out process and can be valuable even when you get to the BOL. As the saying goes, better to have it and not need it than need it and not have it.

I don't suggest that you try to pack ALL of this; there are a number of options in most sections and not all will apply to your circumstances.

Note that some of these items, particularly in the Shelter and Defence sections, might be unlawful to have in a public place during normal times.

Essential documents kit

Shelter. From a choice of:
Tent
Shelter making materials and tools, inc:
Bivvy Sheets
Hammock/Jungle bed

Axe/Kukri/Machete/Hatchet/Big knife
Folding saw/Bow saw/Wire saw
Nylon cord
Bungees
Karabiners/stocking hangers
Mosquito nets
Tent pegs

Bedding inc:
Hammock or jungle bed
Sleeping bags
Insulating mats
Air beds
Blankets
Inflatable pillows

Fire making kit inc:
Lighters
Matches – and suitable containers
Ferro rods
Candles
Fire lighters/jellied fuel/hexamine blocks/cotton wool and Vaseline
Flint and steel sets
Friction tubes

Cooking/eating kit inc:
Stove burning Gas/petrol/paraffin/meths/solid fuel/jelly fuel/wood
Pan set
Kettle
Pan holders
Pan hooks and hangers
Cooking implements
Plates
Bowls

KFS
Mugs
Dish soap
Cloths/scourers

Food and drink inc:
Ration packs/tinned/dried
meats/vegetables/pasta/complete meals
Drinks – coffee/tea/powdered drinks/hot
chocolate/soups
Sweeteners and whiteners
Chocolate/mint cake/other sweets
Jerky
Nuts
Dried fruits
Multivitamins
Alcohol
Snares
Fishing kit – rod, reel, line, hooks, floats, sinkers, nets,
spring hooks or reels,
Guns, ammunition, cleaning kit
Bow or crossbow and arrows/bolts + spare strings
Catapult (slingshot) and ammunition
Skinning/cleaning knife
Sharpening stone
Plant identification book

Water inc:
Bottles of water
Filters and Purifiers
Milbank bags
Chemical purifiers e.g. chlorine tablets/iodine/potassium
permanganate/bleach
Still
Solar and vegetation stills
Desalinators

Light inc:
Torches
Lamps
Candles
Light sticks
Flares
Solar panel and light

Navigation inc:
GPS
Compass
Romer
Map measurer
Hand wound or self winding watch
Pace counter
Sextant
Maps
Map case
Waterproof notebook
Space pen
Pencils with erasers

Signalling and messaging inc:
Personal Locator Beacon
Parachute flares
Fluorescent material
Heliograph
Whistles
Radios
Mobile phones
Emergency charger
Waterproof paper
Marker pen

Clothes inc:
Change of footwear

Spare socks
Thermal layer
Spare T shirt
Light trousers/shorts
Spare underwear
Fleece jacket
Woollen hat
Gloves or mittens
Waterproofs
Boot/shoe brushes and polish or dubbing
Sewing kit

Medical and Hygiene:
Personal medication
First aid kit
Field dressings
Suture kit
Rehydration kit
Other medical items according to your skills and needs
Insect repellent and antihistamine
Soap & shampoo
Towel
Toothbrush and paste, floss
Razors
Comb/brush
Tampons, etc

Tools inc:
Sheath knife
Pocket knife/Multi-tool
Solar charger
Hand-wound charger

Defence inc:
Night vision aid
PIR local area alarms

Extending baton
Guns and ammo

NBCR kit: - masks, gloves, suits, disposable ponchos, over-boots, shoe covers, goggles, monitors, dosimeters, detector paper, fullers earth,

Kits for Kids

I'd guess that most of you expect that you and/or another adult would be around and carrying most stuff to look after yourselves and the kids.

However, to both ease the burden on you and give youngsters a sense of responsibility, they should have their own pack too and it should include some things in case they get separated from you.

What they carry does depend on the capability, maturity and training of the individual child but it comes down to 2 things: what they can reasonably be expected to carry and what they can/you want them to be able to do. So include choices from:

Something in which to carry the kit:
Backpack to suit age and size

Things to alert/contact you if they are separated from you and/or are in trouble:
Their name and emergency contact details for you in a marked and sealed poly bag and/or a bracelet/badge/pendant with those details
Some money and coins (for them or their finder to use to contact you)
Whistle
PMR (mobile phone might be more entertaining and longer range but the network might be down and, even if

warned not to, some kids will breach OpSec and waste the battery calling friends or playing games/music)
Orange/red glow stick
Torch
Note pad
Pencil with eraser (fairly soft lead e.g. 2B)

Things to keep them warm and dry:
Lightweight poncho
Warm hat
Scarf
Gloves

Things to keep them from being hungry or thirsty:
Snacks to their taste
Water
Their own mug, plate/bowl and Knife Fork Spoon set

Things to keep them clean and healthy:
Toothbrush and paste
Tissues
Cleansing wipes
Mini First Aid Kit e.g. insect repellent, antiseptic cream, and plasters
Any personal meds/aids (for younger kids: in a sealed bag marked with details of the child's illness and the medication type and dosage, for administration by others if the kids are separated from you)

Things to keep them happy (according to age)
Favourite cuddly toy
Compact non-electronic game
Book

Bigger/better trained kids might have the above items, plus:

Multi-blade penknife

Compass

Better waterproofs

Poncho/tarp

Cordage

Groundsheet

Sleeping kit e.g. sleeping bag/blanket

Stove

Fire kit

Candle

Mess tin(s)

Two days' simple/light rations

Water bottle

Drink flavouring with energy/vitamin additives

Water purifier or filter bag and puritabs

Wash kit

Toilet paper

FAK

Change of clothes (underclothes and socks as a minimum)

Spare batteries

Survival cards/instructions

Contact details for family or trusted friends and emergency services

Caches

Caches can serve as a supply of some of the items you might otherwise have to take with you, or as additional resources or as replacements for things you use/lose/have stolen on the way. You can place them at or close to a BOL, or at points about a day's travel apart – by your expected form of transport - along the route. Or you can use them for hidden supplies at your home location or BOL so that looters or raiders don't take everything you have.

The contents of a cache will vary according to where it is placed and the things you might need at that location. In case one is found you might split the contents among several smaller containers concealed around the area. Caches for security at a fixed location are covered in Bugging In, so in this book we will look at those for BOLs and resupply between locations.

Each cache needs to be safe from water ingress, vermin, accidental damage and unauthorised discovery.

At your place of work

I will deal with this first because it is probably the easiest.

Usually a cache is kept at work in case you are caught there overnight. This most often happens due to bad weather or a transport failure but could also be due to a nearby terrorist incident or industrial accident that results in local roads being closed. It will rarely need to supply you for more than 48 hours and usually no more than one night.

However, if you have included your workplace as a potential BOL then you may want to extend the quantities or scope of items suggested below.

Except in exceptional circumstances, the items needed are more a matter of comfort than survival and what you include depends on what facilities are available in your building. If you are not strictly confined to the building you might be able to make a brief excursion to a local shop or book in at a nearby hotel and have even more comfort but even then a few personal items will be welcome.

You could keep this kit in your car if you can park very close by, but better still, because you might not be able to get to the car, you could stash it in a locker or desk drawer. Some of it might be included as a part of your EDC, especially if you carry items in a bag in addition to those in your pockets. Some might be available from the resources at work, in which case you don't need to include your own.

For our purposes let's assume a worst case scenario, and accept that if things are better than this then you have a bonus. So: you are confined to your workplace; the power is off; communications i.e. landline and mobile phones are out; all your colleagues have decided to risk the journey, so you are on your own.

You should discuss this scenario in advance with your family. If you are not home by the time they expect you and they cannot contact you by phone or email, they should turn on the news to look for reports of what might have happened where you are. Similarly, you should tune in to the news to find out how wide the area is that is affected. Both of you should then know that the other is prepared for this eventuality, knows what to do and has the resources that they need, so that you are not unduly worried, nor tempted to take what would be unnecessary risks trying to reach one another.

The workplace cache should keep you from being: cold; uncomfortable; hungry; thirsty; bored; or frightened.

Any workplace should provide:
Toilet facilities
Water, soap and towels for hand washing
First aid kit
Drinking water
There could also be many resources that you could adapt, such as curtains for blankets and stuffing from seats for

insulation, but remember that when/if things return to normal you will have to explain what you have done! Now, lock yourself in and then pull out your personal cache.

For these circumstances you might want to have available:
Supply of any personal medications
Warm hat, gloves, socks, jumper or fleece
Washing/tooth cleaning/shaving kit
Wind up radio
Wind up or battery lamp, or candles (which will also provide some heat)
Torch – head torches are excellent for these situations
Book, e-reader, crosswords or other puzzles, or films on disk if you have a laptop computer or personal DVD player
Small gas stove
Spare canister of gas
Lighter
Pan or mess tin
Mug
Spoon
Food including biscuits and other snacks plus boil-in-the-bag meals
Tea/coffee/hot chocolate + sugar and milk powder if required

This kit doesn't cost a lot or take up much space but if you need it you'll be glad you've got it.

With family/friends/caravan/boat
This is pretty much a repeat of the short-term local area kit, except because you don't have to carry it you can include more food and other consumables. For all the other items you could rely on arriving with your STLA kit intact or if you know that the BOL is well equipped you could cache

consumables plus personal wash kit – toothbrush, paste, brush, razor, etc – some personals meds, a change of clothes, and anything extra for children or pets.

This should satisfy your emergency personal needs and, if you are staying with family or friends, ensure you do not stretch their preps. You can stash these items in locked bags or boxes wherever the property owner has room for them. On a boat or caravan put them out of sight and in a place not easy to access and then cover or camouflage them to look like part of the structure or basic systems of the vehicle.

At a higher level, we have some friends who live on a rural small holding. There are selected others who will go to them if a major Event occurs. Since in that situation they expect that the Bug Out might be a permanent move and all residents will operate as part of a survival group, each member caches much more than I have suggested above. In fact each member of the group initially contributes at least a 1 year supply of food and other items to the communal stores and gradually builds that to 2 years. These are all selected for long storage life, packed in air-tight containers with oxygen displacers and dehumidifiers and hidden or buried.

Since the stores are communal, it is agreed in advance what a member will contribute, though they may add personal favourites to the stock if they so wish. Each member will also contribute some specialist skill(s) and cache appropriate tools and resources for use with those skills. This set-up is beyond the perceived needs of most Preppers in the UK but it is not uncommon among the most serious and well prepared.

Hotel, B&B, Camp site

Because these sites are constantly in use by others and regularly worked and altered by the owners, it is not usually possible to establish a cache on site. It might be that in the circumstances you expect to use such a BOL you wouldn't actually need a cache and if you arrived with little in hand you could then shop for whatever you didn't have.

However, if you do perceive a need, you can sometimes find a location nearby that does not look as though it will be disturbed and where you can establish a cache or where you can do some guerrilla planting.

Urban sites

Urban sites that you don't own are particularly risky for a long term cache because of the likelihood that the council or owners of any derelict building will demolish it and bulldoze the land before rebuilding or turning it to other use.

If you do decide to plant a cache, the contents should be inexpensive simple items such as: basics for fire starting, rat traps and home-made catapult for food gathering, or car boot sale tools to help affect entry and improvisation e.g. a crowbar, hacksaw, or bolt croppers.

Site the cache where you can both place and recover it unobserved, preferably near the boundary of the property since that might be one of the last areas to be disturbed and where you have best chance of recovering it if you see signs of development on the site.

Use a container that is unremarkable if found; a length of external water pipe capped at each end is good and better if you enclose it in a longer length of clay sewerage pip then bury it. Most people won't want to investigate that too closely if they accidentally uncover it.

Otherwise pack the contents carefully and then enclose them in a sound but cosmetically battered metal can or other piece of rubbish and dump it among similar abandoned items. Make sure you can identify it from its fellows even after weathering.

Wilderness BOLs

Caches on or near well sited wilderness BOLs are undoubtedly the most secure of the genre. In fact they can be so secure that if the location is not chosen carefully and detailed notes kept on how to find it, you might never again see the contents!

Classic location notes usually feature a landmark, either a second landmark or a compass bearing or both, a paced distance and sometimes additional helpful information.

e.g. OS85GR333658 Pylon W leg 253° 27 paces. Under rocks.

That is the OS map number 85, the six figure grid reference 333658, at which point you will find a pylon as a landmark. From the westerly leg of the pylon, take a bearing of 253 degrees magnetic, and walk out 27 paces. At that point look or dig under a pile of rocks to find the cache.

I have seen caches sited by use of a GPS, as they are for the recreational activity of Geocaching but I dislike the dependence on technical systems for use in times of disruption. GPS makes you reliant on the satellites still being operational and transmitting accurate information, and on a battery powered device working properly. The old fashioned method requires a piece of paper, a map and a compass. Less to go wrong = more reliable.

The best containers are waterproof sealed plastic boxes or tubs. These are usually buried or covered. If you do bury them, ensure that you conceal or can make a suitable digging tool nearby. If you only want to remove the lid and leave the container in place, burying is not a problem but if you want to lift the whole container, place it in two or three polythene bags e.g. rubble sacks, one inside the other. If you don't, after the ground has settled around the container you will be in for a lot of digging! If the ground is frozen you'd have a real problem.

When placing the container, be aware of the potential for shifting ground, falling trees, flooding and other water coursing, and new growth of foliage and weeds that might make it more difficult to find and get to the cache.

A wilderness cache might contain a selection of items that you would normally have in a BOB, including those for:

Building a shelter: big knife/hatchet, tarp, nylon cordage
Fire starting: disposable lighter(s), Ferro rod and striker, cotton wool, candles
Collecting/purifying water: water bottle, Milbank bag, puritabs
Food: dehydrated rations, barley sugar, snares, fishing kit, lock knife, salt
Cooking: metal pot, spoon
Medical: blister kit, clean socks, plasters, bandages, antiseptic cream, antihistamine, insect repellent, etc
Hygiene: toilet paper, wipes, bar of soap, hand sanitiser, toothbrush and paste, comb
Tools: multi tool, sharpening stone, ammunition, local maps, compass, notepad and pencil

Wayside caches

It can be difficult to determine the correct placing for wayside caches. If you plan to drive between home and a distant BOL, 300 miles without a stop is not difficult. Three hundred miles on foot could take two to three weeks. For the car you don't need a cache en route. Walking you would ideally have one every day or two for resupply, and the route might be very different from the one you would drive. If you managed to drive half way before having to abandon the car, half of the caches would be wasted. If you didn't drive that far, you might need all of them. So what do you do?

Accept that you can never know for sure exactly what the situation is going to be or require and that any source of supply you might have is better than none.

Consider carefully each of your intended routes to different BOLs using differing methods of transport. Although you will have chosen the ways least likely to be blocked, look for the possible hazards that might cause you to change your route or to move from one form of travel to another.

Travel those routes and identify the existing sources of supply, including: shops and garages; fields with crops or domestic animals; fish farms; rivers; garden ponds; rabbit warrens; deer in fields; roadside signs advertising eggs, honey, or other home produce; useful wild plants; farms, firms, or houses with diesel or domestic oil tanks; allotments and productive gardens; barns or other buildings that might be used for shelter; bunkers with coal or piles of peat; water barrels; basically anything that you might be able to make use of if you are in need.

When you have identified these existing potential sources of supply, note which ones you might be able to approach to offer payment and which you might be able to access after dark. Look for security lights and signs of dogs around the property.

Locate or cache equipment that will help you to access those resources. Then in areas that seem barren of these supplies look for places you might be able to establish a food cache that stands a reasonable chance of remaining intact.

For your cache you want somewhere that looks undisturbed such as scrubby weeds, in rough terrain, away from any visible power lines or water courses, just over a fence. This is unlikely to be disturbed by the land owner, the roads department, or utility companies. Ensure you can plant and recover your cache unobserved and with consideration of all the factors I mentioned in the previous section.

The container can be similar to that for wilderness or for urban areas but do ensure you can find it again after you have planted it!

In conclusion:
1)   Different bug-out situations demand differing types and levels of equipment.

2)   You can develop individual options or adapt a modular approach, with each level forming part of a more comprehensive kit.

3)   Whatever the contents of a kit, you have to be able to transport it using the type of transport – including your legs and back – that you have available.

4)   Don't forget specialised resources for individual needs, including those of children and pets.

5)   Where practical, caches can be pre-positioned to save you some carrying and extend the variety of items available or to provide for specialised needs or opportunities at a specific location

Bugging Out Task List

- Carry out a threat assessment and decide which events would potentially require you to Bug Out
- Establish the trigger points that would initiate a bug out
- Identify suitable Bug Out Locations (BOLs) for each of the potential scenarios. Select multiple locations in differing directions and at differing distances from your Bug In Location (BIL). Ensure each location would be accessible and provide for your needs when there
- Identify various routes (BORs) to the BOLs. Ensure these do not include any routes that might become blocked by other evacuees unless you intend to leave well before any general evacuation. Select routes for differing forms of transport, including on foot
- Identify the most suitable form of transport for each route and the alternatives
- Make a reconnaissance of each BOL to ensure that it is viable under the situation expected to require its use
- Make a reconnaissance of each route to identify any possible blockage points and detour routes to get around them
- Identify and develop the skills you would need during travel to and after reaching your BOL (That is a short sentence but a lifetime's ongoing task!)
- Identify shelter, resupply (especially water), and possible cache points along each route
- Acquire, or identify a reliable source of, each form of transport you intend to use
- Buy and securely store fuel, spares and other items needed for operation of each form of transport
- Establish RV points close to home and on each route for people not present when the BO is initiated

- Identify and establish message points near each RV and along the route to update followers on progress, any changes, and identified threats
- Establish communication plans, including coded visible messages, so that group members not present at time of evacuation are informed of who has gone, when, and the route taken
- Identify what equipment and supplies you would need for each person in your group, how it would be transported and by whom.
- Buy and pack the equipment and supplies.
- Store the containers where they would be easily and quickly available in the event of a short-notice evacuation
- Use and test each of the items of equipment, under realistic conditions, to ensure they will perform as needed
- Establish caches at suitable locations along the routes to, and where practical at, your BOLs
- Discretely plant edible and medicinal vegetables and herbs along your BORs and around BOLs
- Ensure all members of the group understand the plans, routes and the various stages and requirements
- Develop group and individual skills required
- Regularly review threats, BOLs and BORs adapt as required
- Check and replace equipment and supplies as required
- Develop and maintain skills through regular practise

Leaving home

If you have chance during your final preps or otherwise immediately before you leave the house, you should deal with as many as possible of the items on the following list.

Update your information

You should be constantly monitoring the news and any other sources of information from the instant that you first become aware of a situation that might require you to Bug Out, but ensure you have all the latest updates immediately before you leave.

Dress appropriately

Check the weather now and the forecast for the rest of the day and make sure you are appropriately dressed, with alternatives for as things change.

Underwear and inner socks should be worn-in and comfortable. If it is cold outside, and especially if you won't be walking or using transport that requires physical effort, then you might want to wear a thermal layer. Your basic outer clothing should be tough, with trousers for everybody, male or female, and a work/outdoor shirt. Shoes or boots should also be strong and well worn-in but with plenty of life left. You might need an intermediate layer such as a fleece or jumper. On the outside might be a strong wind and water proof jacket in a muted colour and possibly even trousers to match.

If the Bug Out is in daylight in warm dry weather some of those layers might be left off, but remember this is UK, you could need the warm and waterproof gear five minutes after stepping out of the door, so keep it handy.

Check your kit

Go through your list of kit. Make sure you haven't forgotten anything including essential documents and family photographs. If possible, add anything special required for the current Event that is not already included. Don't forget valuables that are locked in a safe but that you want to take with you.

Top up the tank

Ensure any vehicles are fully fuelled and the oil, radiator, and windscreen wash are at maximum levels. Check the tyres, including the spare, and top up if required. Apply any protective equipment you think might be needed, such as wire netting over the windows (see next chapter for when/not to do this). Make sure any essential tools will be available without having to unload everything else to get at them.

Load up

Pack all your gear and then cover it as well as possible so that it doesn't provide a temptation for anyone who might want to steal it. Prepare and position any defensive equipment for rapid access should you be attacked.

Children and Pets

Children, and pets that you are taking with you, should be given a chance and encouraged to relieve themselves. Fit any appropriate identification. Secure them in their travelling container. Load them onto the transport. Don't forget any medication, food and equipment they will require.

Cats, rodents, birds and large animals such as donkeys or horses you are not taking should be released where they will have a chance to feed and find water. Some will survive, some won't but at least they will have a chance. If you can attach a tag that will identify them as belonging to you do so and you might see them again.

Most dogs or non-native species such as snakes will not

survive, will suffer, and might be a hazard to strangers. Do not confine them and do not release them. They should be put down humanely. Do that outside or take the body there, so that if you do return the house will not be affected by their decomposed remains or the vermin that will prey on them. Bury or cremate the body if you have time.

Take care of your bodily needs
You never know when you will next get the chance!

Switch off utilities
Unplug all appliances from electrical sockets and turn off lights. Turn off the gas and electric at the mains. Flush the toilets and apply bleach. Turn off water at the stop tap on the inlet pipe and drain down both hot and cold water. Start at the top of the house and work your way down, leaving taps open as you go. Close all taps when the water stops flowing.

Secure the house
Lock all doors and windows. If appropriate to the situation and you can, apply window boards or flood defences.

Make contact or Leave messages
Contact other people with whom you will be travelling and arrange to meet. Contact family members or friends to let them know you are leaving. If possible contact anyone to whose location you are bugging out; to let them know you are on the way. If you have a pre-arranged system of coded messages to let anyone who comes looking for you know where you have gone and when you left, set them in place now.

Final look and photographs
Take a last look at the place, check nobody has forgotten anything, and take a final photograph for insurance or other purposes. Leave.

How to survive

In this chapter I don't intend to try to teach you how to use a map and compass or build a brush shelter or set a figure four trap release; there are already plenty of outdoor survival books that will give you that information.

Instead I will concentrate on the topics that those other books don't cover; information on keeping yourself safe as you Bug Out.

Much of this will come from my military background but I don't expect you to have the resources or training that the Armed Forces do, so I have adapted it to the civilian context and particularly to the terrain and circumstances you are most likely to encounter in the UK. If you are one of my readers overseas, please adjust these details to your environment and culture and if you have any specific questions feel free to contact me via the email address given at the end of this book.

Most emergency situations you are liable to face will be relatively local and won't involve a complete breakdown of society but fear and confusion can make some people act in ways that would normally be out of character for them. That can include them acting dishonestly and/or aggressively. Even so, you probably won't need to take more precautions than you should when walking through any part of a city, but especially one you don't know. For example:

Stay alert to people and events around you. Don't wander along chatting into your super latest mobile phone, texting, playing games, or with plugs in your ears listening to music.

If you want to tune in to a weather or news update or to make/receive a call: find a place to stop where you have something solid at your back and on at least one side, where you are not obvious but can see what is going on around you; put an earphone in ONE ear; and remain alert while listening.

Stay only as long as you must. When you are finished or if anyone approaches your position, put away your phone/radio and move on.

Don't display property, or your body, in ways that might attract unwanted attention.

Blend in with your surroundings; adapt your clothing, posture, movement, baggage, and reaction to other people, to fit.

If you have an injury, handicap or weakness that might make you seem vulnerable, hide or disguise it.

Unless it makes you stand out unduly in your present environment, walk upright; make your posture and movement display confidence. Show that you belong where you are and know exactly where you are going.

Know how to defend yourself, verbally or physically, and be prepared to do so if required.

Be especially alert near to home or in other areas where you feel comfortable; otherwise you will relax and let down your guard and consequently be at your most vulnerable.

I know not all of that is politically correct, but survival isn't a PC endeavour!

For the remainder of this chapter, we will consider disasters that cover a wider area and a more general breakdown in normal rules of behaviour. Remember that, whatever your plans, you might have to use both the information for travelling by vehicle and on foot at various stages of your journey, and some of it is transferable, especially if you are using a bike or horse rather than a car or truck. Use any as your situation requires at the time and tone it down if things aren't that bad. Either way, the information is there.

Movement plans

When making any plans for a Bug Out, the Rule of Three applies. In this case the rule is that you should identify three different forms of transport and three different routes. In that way, if your primary choice of transport or route isn't available you can fall back on the next.

You should not simply pick these routes from a map and leave it at that. Having chosen the paths you should travel each of them, preferably using the relevant method(s) of transport, so that you know they are viable. Actually doing it will reveal many things that you will miss or not know from a map or satellite images. It is while doing this reconnaissance that you can also survey for resources and sites for any caches along the route.

For example your ideal method of transport might be your 4x4 but a multiple car pile up just along the road means no large vehicle can get past or around the wreckage, so you go to plan B and change to the bicycles. You set off along your chosen route but soon find that flooding is blocking the road, so you get out your maps, find a way from where you are to your secondary route and proceed from there. Options are good things and identifying and checking them in advance gives confidence in a time of stress.

When overseas I have sometimes extended this so that I chose three exits by sea e.g. commercial passenger ship, passage on a cargo vessel, hire of a boat; then three by air e.g. commercial flight, charter flight, private hire; and three by land e.g. private vehicle, bus, walking; with different exit points, initial destinations, and routes for each. The more choices you have, the surer one will work.

Each member of your team or group should know and understand these plans. For events that prevent some members being with you when you have to leave, you should have a number of pre-planned rendezvous and message points along the way.

One of these will be close to home, others further away. Near to each there should be a message point where you can leave a coded message of when you left, where you have gone, and any other essential information. This can be in a hidden container or disguised as graffiti on a wall or the back of a road sign. If not before, your missing members should eventually join you at your ultimate destination.

Route planning

Route planning isn't so much something you do after selecting a BOL as a part of it. Remember that when you are making your choices two of the things to look for are that the BOL is off the main roads and accessible even if those routes are blocked.

You should also be checking for possible blockage points along even your less-travelled route and for potential ambush sites where desperate survivors might try to hold you up in order to steal your transport and other resources. And of course you ensure the route is practical for your chosen form of transport.

This might take you on a long, circuitous path but that should not be a problem if it helps you to reach your destination safely.

Individuals or small teams on foot

The tactics and principles of movement and defence for someone on their own or part of a small team when bugging out are akin to those of a soldier having to escape and evade or a reconnaissance team in potentially hostile territory.

Your main advantage is that although you might have competition from human predators you are unlikely to have to evade large groups of people actively tracking you, or worry about aircraft or other high-tech detection equipment, though dogs might still be a problem.

In this environment you have to look to your security both while on the move and at halts. I cannot give you a full course in fieldcraft or E&E in this book, but some hints and tips might help.

On the Move: Your protection on the move while bugging out on foot comes down to two things: alertness and choice of route. For both you have to remember that your aim is to see but not to be seen and things are seen because of: shape, silhouette, shine, shadow, spacing, and movement. They can otherwise be detected at a distance by sound or smell.

The human shape is both specific and well known to other humans and animals and, unfortunately for these purposes, not particularly similar to anything much else in the environment. That makes us stand out and is one of the reasons we are easy targets. To overcome that, you have to use other objects to disguise your shape so that you blend in. One way to do that is to put yourself behind, or if other aspects are taken care of, in front of, something that will hide your shape such as a bush in the rural environment or a car or rubbish skip in town. In order to stay hidden as you move you can either move from one piece of cover to another or you can dress in something that breaks up your shape so that it resembles something in the environment through which you are moving, or both.

Snipers do this by wearing a Ghillie Suit, which has netting covered in pieces of Hessian or plastic that resemble leaves. They then extend that by adding pieces of real foliage, grass, or other plants to further blend to their surroundings. In an urban situation they might hide in a rubbish pile and cover themselves with strips or pieces of black plastic bin liner, supermarket carrier bags, etc. When standing you need to extend this all around the body, when lying down, the head is particularly important and when sitting or kneeling the head and shoulders.

I'm not suggesting that you go into full sniper mode, but it is something you should know about and using cover and concealment when either moving or at rest is an important factor in staying safe.

Silhouette is an extension of shape; it is simply a situation in which your shape is highlighted even more than normal. It occurs whenever you are in front of a lighter background, be that a wall, the sky, artificial lights, or a body of water. You don't have to do anything to yourself to deal with this, just be aware of it happening and avoid it. For example if you have to cross the brow of a hill, do it close beside a line of bushes or a stone wall and keep your head below the top of the cover. If you have to cross a wall or other obstacle, roll or crawl over it if possible rather than jumping or clambering. If you have to move in front of lights crawl across or move behind cars.

Shine is the reflection of light. Culprits on your body might include things such as your watch, jewellery, fastenings on your pack or luggage, and the like but also very light areas of skin such as your face and hands. To hide these you can either cover them with fabric or apply dirt or charcoal. If you use skin colouring, apply it in wide streaks that run at an angle to the normal plane of that area of skin e.g. diagonally across the forehead in a wave pattern rather straight across or up and down. In a built up area with a lot of concrete use grey coloured dust that matches the surroundings. In any disaster, whether you are in town or country, nobody is going to be surprised if you are dirty. Not that they should see you anyway!

For our purposes shine also includes colour and form. If you want to blend, then in the countryside you wear camouflage pattern or natural colours such as muted shades of green and brown. In the city you want dark colours but in the style other people in the area are wearing, be that a suit, tie and bowler or a hoodie and jeans.

If you can't avoid being seen, be unattractive, with nothing worth stealing. Adapt your clothes and luggage so you look like one of the long-term homeless rather than a new member of that clan.

Shadow can help to conceal you if you hide in it, but if you stand behind something and a light casts your shadow to the side, that can give you away. If you are in a position for a while, remember that the sun and moon move relative to your position and shadow that hid you or was not cast by you might move in the opposite direction until you are exposed or revealed.

In nature, equal spacing is rare and anything that has it tends to stand out. In places that are man-made exactly the opposite is true and an oddity in the sequence of objects will catch our eye. This is something to bear in mind if you are moving or observing as a team. Don't stand or walk the same distance apart, unless in an urban setting you are simulating a continuation of an existing sequence of something,

But even with all of those things covered, wearing a perfect Ghillie suit, nothing shining, behind natural cover, etc, the one thing that stands out more than anything is movement and you are certainly going to have to move at times. The key then is to either move very slowly or to move in the way and at the speed things around you are moving, be that wind blown foliage, animals, or, in the city, other people.

You must also minimise the noise you make. Before each step, look and feel for anything that could make noise e.g. puddles, dry sticks or vegetation, gravel, dry leaves, etc. Devise a system of hand signals you can all understand, so that you can communicate silently. You don't need to use standard military signals but you can if you prefer that to making up your own.

Having learnt the things that can give you away and how to overcome them, you then have to realise that the same is true for anyone that might have bad intentions towards you.

As you move and particularly before you leave cover and move into an open space, you must stop and search the surroundings for any of those giveaways that might reveal an enemy. A small but good quality pair of binoculars or a monocular is an extremely valuable piece of survival equipment in this situation and one you would do well to add to your kit list. Many of the things that would give you away can also be hidden by moving in darkness but to give you the edge by letting you see other people, a night vision scope or goggles is a major, if expensive, advantage.

When a small civilian team moves it should do so in one of a few formations: line i.e. one behind the other; arrowhead i.e. one at the front and one either side a bit further back; or diamond if there are four or more of you. The military have a lot more formations than that but they are used in accordance with the weaponry available and for the situations they might face in battle. The ones I mentioned will give you good visibility all round and a chance to respond quickly to a threat from any direction. You should be no less than ten yards apart but remember to vary that spacing.

Perhaps one other formation you might use is line abreast i.e. beside one another, when you are crossing a junction of roads or tracks. If you adopt this and run across the junction together you are least exposed, don't give anyone a chance to attack someone following the first they see cross, and it helps to hide how many of you there are.

When you move do so slowly, stop regularly to look, listen and smell for any signs of other people. Looking and listening are obvious but you can often smell wood smoke, food cooking, or in close country body odour, scents, or insect repellent, or you might hear people moving or as they carry out various tasks, before you see them.

Note the lines and places to which your eyes are naturally drawn e.g. along tunnel effects such a woodland tracks or to particularly dark places that might hide a predator, then deliberately move your attention to the other places so as not to miss anything.

Before you move out of cover, scan the ground ahead in zones; first the most distant line you can see, then the middle distance, and finally the area of most immediate threat – every detail of the next one hundred yards or so.

Occasionally, when you come to a place where a change of direction will be hidden, move off your line of movement and loop around back the way you came. Find a place where you can hide and stop for a while to watch for anyone following you. If there is anyone, you have choices. You could challenge or attack them, but be aware that they might just be the scout/tracker for a larger party coming behind them. Or you could wait until they are past and then either follow them to determine their intentions or you might head off in a different direction to the one you were going, until you can be sure you are no longer being tracked.

Actual movement

The Walk: When moving tactically you have to suit the method to the ground and situation. If you can walk upright, then do so slowly, stopping every few paces to look, listen, smell, and sense any enemy. Constantly look for places where you can take cover, and for escape routes. At each stop, study every potential hiding or ambush point, every place that might conceal an attacker or sniper, looking for all the things we covered that might give you away to others but that might now reveal them to you. When you are satisfied you can detect no threat, and that you know where to go if one is revealed, move on.

Look too for obstacles and other potential threats to your movement including: debris, damaged or otherwise unsafe flooring, loose or noisy materials underfoot or in your path. As you step forward, do so about half your normal length of pace. Watch your balance but keep your weight slightly backwards. Be ready to step over or around even small obstacles, especially if they might conceal hidden dangers. Place your foot, little toe down first, roll inwards onto your toes and then slowly lower your heel, constantly alert for the crunch of dirt or gravel, the creaking of a floorboard or unseen twig, or other noise that might alert someone. Be ready to freeze at the first sign of trouble and then lift your foot carefully before finding a better place to put it down. As you move forward, watch for any change of light, any opening or other place that might reveal you, and be prepared to move into one of the other methods of movement given below.

The run: In these situations you only run when you have no other choice. If you are running to escape from danger then just RUN but watch constantly for anything that could cause a slip or trip that might slow you down and give you to what you were fleeing, or cause you damage from the fall.

But the other time you run is if there is no other reasonable option but to cross open ground and no cover behind which you can crawl. In this case you should use all your concentration to detect any potential threat while you are exposed and look for ways to minimise the danger. If possible wait for a distraction e.g. a loud noise from a direction away from the ground you must cross, or cloud over the sun or moon, and then cross the ground as quickly as possible but not in Chariots of Fire fashion, head back and arms pumping; run hunched to make yourself as small a target as possible, get into cover as soon as possible, and then move from that cover and as far away as fast as you can, preferably in a direction away from your line of travel as you crossed the open ground. If there is a chance of somebody shooting at you, jink and weave as you run, make sudden stops and faster spurts, dives and rolls, to make it more difficult for them to know where to aim. When somebody who knows what they are doing shoots at a moving target, they don't aim where it is, they aim where it will be when the bullet arrives; you have to make it as difficult as possible for them to predict that. If there is a group of you, run together, bunched, You make a larger target but only one chance for someone to spot and take a shot at you.

The Monkey Run: The monkey run is a fast, four point of contact crawl used to cross areas where there is approximately waist high cover. For this you 'run' on your toes or knees and knuckles; the latter to prevent possible damage to your fingers and palms. Watch where you are going but keep your head low. Although it slows you down a little and is hard on the back, remember to keep your backside down - it can save you from getting it shot off!

The Cossack Crawl: This is a sort of sideways shuffle with one leg extended to help your balance while you are otherwise facing at roughly right angles to your line of movement. It is usually used to navigate broken cover while watching a potential threat point. It is a position you can move from quickly into either a crawl or a run in any direction.

The Roll: The roll can be used to escape downhill. In this case you lock your legs straight and together, your arms by your sides clutching your clothing or crossed at the front, and roll sideways. It can be fast but is potentially dangerous if you hit any hidden obstacles. Otherwise it is used to cover ground behind low cover more quickly than with a sideways crawl. It is also a way to minimise your profile while crossing a flat-topped obstacle such as a wall but you should always check what is on the other side of the obstacle before crossing. Broken glass, rubble, or spikes, a longer drop than on the side where you mounted, or numerous other potential dangers might lurk unseen. A mirror is a good aid for a covert check for hazards but it doesn't help much if the far side is in darkness, so take care.

The Crawl: Forwards, sideward, or backwards, it is flat on your belly, shuffling along using your forearms and legs for propulsion. The crawl is slow and incredibly tiring (try it for a hundred yards or so if you've never done it!) but it can keep you below the level of cover, out of sight or gunshot, to allow you to either evade or creep up on an enemy. Shift as much gear as you can from your pockets or bags to your side – not your back - so as to keep your body low and avoid raising even gear above the cover while also preventing damage to you, your clothes or your stuff.

The Ghost Walk: Right, admit it, who among you wanted to play at being a zombie? Well this is your chance, and in the dark too! This is the first of 3 movement styles that are usually, though not exclusively, used at night. Of course if you do it right then nobody will ever see you or know you are there but maybe that isn't a bad thing.

The ghost walk is the method used to feel your way in almost complete darkness without the aid of night vision goggles. The technique really is like a zombie walk, upright with both hands extended forward, waving slowly about feeling for obstructions, while you do the same with each foot at a time to identify low level obstructions before putting the foot down. Gradually squat and come back up feeling with your hands to ensure there is nothing in front of you at any height.

The advice I was given was, 'Imagine there is someone in front of you that you really fancy, they are naked and you are trying to explore every inch of their body, and with every step you take forward they step back for you to do it again!' This was long before I met my wife and no, I'm not saying who the lady of my imagination was!

The temptation is to look down or straight forward but if you can find any lighter background in front of or above you then you can silhouette potential obstacles and help to keep direction. This works particularly well if trying to follow a track or path between trees or buildings, so look up, feel down!

The Cat Walk: The Cat Walk is another all-fours crawl, but is done much more slowly than the monkey run. In this case you move forwards feeling the ground with one hand at a time and removing debris or anything else that might make a noise before putting it down. You then bring the knee on that side forwards and place it where your hand was, before then moving the other hand. If done correctly, this is a slow but very quiet method of movement and it gives you plenty of opportunity to use all your senses to detect any threat.

The Kitten Crawl: This is used for moving low, slow, and very quiet. You begin flat on your front, search the ground before you with your fingers and then bring your hands back level with your chest, place your hands palms down, raise your body from the ground on your hands and toes, move your torso forwards, lower it, bring your toes forward, and then repeat, You move only a few inches each time, so this is not the way to cover ground quickly, but it is not a tiring exercise and is probably the most covert of all the movement styles.

Choice of route: when moving through hill country you won't be walking over the hills, you will be walking among them. And when walking through woods you won't be using tracks unless the vegetation is so thick you have no choice, though you might parallel them to ease navigation.

When choosing your route you won't usually be looking for the quickest or the easiest path. Speed can sometimes be important but safety is always more so. What you will be looking for is a way that gives you cover, but doesn't offer the same advantage to a would-be attacker.

You won't walk over the hills because that would silhouette you against the sky. You will avoid tracks because that is where other people will walk and where thieves will target an ambush.

So, in hilly but otherwise open country the best place to move whenever practical is about a third of the way up the side of the hill. This will also help you to avoid the boggy ground that is often in the base of a valley or cutting.

As you move, constantly look for places where predators might be hiding and be ready to avoid them.

In woodland, where possible avoid tracks and move among the trees, for the same reasons as you would in open areas but also because it will give better cover for movement and to quickly hide if you need to.

In urban areas use alleys, lanes, parks, derelict sites,

alongside railway lines rivers or canals, or even through gardens rather than following the main thoroughfares. In parks apply the same rules that you would in the countryside.

These lines of travel are generally harder work and slower but safer than regular pathways.

Rest stops: whenever you stop, move into an area of thick cover, preferably backed by dense shadow, which will hide you from view but still allow you to see around you. Moving through the cover should mean that anyone less stealthy than you will make noise that will alert you to their approach. Under fallen trees in an area of similar wind damage is often good, but make sure you have a concealed escape path should it be needed.

If you are alone this choice is especially important. If you have stopped to sleep, eat or take care of other needs, your attention will be diverted. After you get into the cover, sit and wait, watching for any followers or other threat. Only when you are sure you are secure should you relax enough to do whatever you want to do here.

If you have companions, at least one should always be on watch while others take care of the administrative tasks or begin to rest. When someone has eaten, been to the toilet, slept, or whatever, they can take watch while the sentry takes their turn to relax.

If there are three or four of you, two on watch while the other(s) rest/sleep gives a better chance that at least one of the guards will stay awake.

If you erect a shelter, keep the roof low. This both helps concealment and minimises heat loss, but you must have room under the cover to get off the ground to avoid damp and cold, using either an insulating mat or a bough bed. If you must cut foliage, take low branches from the side of trees opposite to any likely line of approach and rub soil onto the stub where you cut the branch. If you cut bracken, take it from the centre of patches not the edges and don't take it all from one place. Take either branches or undergrowth from as far as practical from your resting point.

If you need to cook or heat water, use a stove if you have  fuel. If you must have a wood fire then keep it small and burn only dry inner wood, to minimise light and smoke.

If you are in an urban area the same principles apply, only your materials will be different.

Most importantly, when either on the move or at stops, remember that this is no longer practise. You are not camping or hill walking or playing at bushcraft; you are trying to survive in a hostile environment where every choice and movement can make the difference as to whether you live or not.

Movement in groups

If you are on your own or with others in a single vehicle then movement is simplified but if you are travelling in/on more than one vehicle and want to arrive together then you need some organisation. Basically you need a convoy.

The more familiar members of your group are with emergency procedures and the more often you practise them the less planning you will need in an emergency. That said, you don't always know who will gather and want to travel together, so procedures might have to be adapted to fit.

Depending on the urgency of the situation you might use a quick briefing or, if time permits, a more detailed briefing.

In a **Quick Briefing** you agree:
Destination
Preferred route

Who and what goes in what vehicle
Order of travel
Method of communication

What happens on the journey is then either Standard Operating Procedure (SOP) if you are a well-practised team or 'make it up as you go along' if there is no time for anything else.

If you have the opportunity for detailed planning then there should be a detailed discussion/briefing in advance of preparing vehicles and loads and a quick meeting for any questions and to confirm the main points before you leave. The lists below contain headings taken from standard military convoy orders but omit elements not relevant to a civilian group. Before you reject this as overly complex, remember that it is based on generations of operational experience of what works, what goes wrong, and how to survive and complete your journey even if things don't work as hoped.

The military have another principle: 'No plan of battle survives first contact with the enemy' i.e. nobody can plan for everything and what can go wrong probably will. However, planning for what you can and improvising when you have to gives a much greater chance of success than making it all up as you go and hoping for the best.

Maps will be helpful in explaining the route and if you can issue pre-printed route cards then they will be useful. The navigator/front seat passenger in each vehicle should attend and bring a notebook, a pen, and a map.

If GPS is working, anyone who has one can set it up later but emphasise that the route briefed has priority and must be followed. GPS should only be used if the owner gets separated and can't find their way from the directions agreed.

Having some paper, pens, and spare maps available for anyone that doesn't bring one saves time that would be lost while they go to look for their own. After the lists below, there is much more detail on the information that should be included in each of the specific topics and the procedures that should be followed.

A **Detailed Briefing** should contain:

Situation:
An update on the situation causing you to Bug Out
Any known developments, such as the extent of the area affected
Who is travelling with you or going their own way

Execution:
Destination
Timings: time of departure; expected time of arrival; time of any stops e.g. for comfort breaks/meals/refuelling/etc, end of first day's journey (if more than one)
Order of travel
Route(s) – roads, junctions, points to note
Spacing of vehicles
Speed
Loading of vehicles; who and what
Defence on the move – staying safe
Halts – where, when, for how long, who does what
Lights
Actions on:
Blocked route
Breakdown
Separation
Getting lost
Official roadblock
Unofficial roadblock
Illness
Attack

Support:
Special equipment, supplies and skills – who, what, where
Feeding and water

Signals:
Headlights
Horn
Radios

Any questions:
In the military they do this at the end of Orders. You might allow for them as you go through the briefing. That's your choice but if things devolve into a discussion or argument it can seriously extend the session.

Execution topics
Timings: the time of departure should be fixed and absolutely adhered to; otherwise every other timing is potentially thrown out. To give the best chance of departing on time, allow plenty of leeway for the tasks that have to be done before that.

Give everyone a copy of the pages from the chapter 'Leaving Home', so that they have a process to follow and are less likely to forget or have to repeat things. You might be on the road for a while before your first stop and people will be nervous, so the sections on everyone taking care of bodily needs are especially important!

If the group isn't sufficiently organised for all tasks to be allocated and coordinated, then encourage the more efficient members to help others after they have finished their own preparations to leave.

After you are underway there are many things that can affect whether you can adhere to the other timings. Keep them realistically in line with distances and expected speeds but do allow some stretch. If you are ahead of time you can always extend breaks a little, which is usually appreciated. If you fall behind then you can try to catch up by increasing speed or reducing breaks. Do what you have to do.

Order of Travel: Depending on the type and number of vehicles you have in your convoy you might have:

The Scout – This could be a light, responsive car or a motorcycle. If you are all on motorbikes, bicycles, horses, or foot, then one or two of the fastest and most experienced in the group would take the role. The scout's job is to go ahead of the main group to look for possible blockages or ambushes. If your way is blocked then it is the Scout's job to reconnoitre a path to an alternative. If you have radios then the priority users for them are the scout and the lead vehicle. To keep the scout light, any heavy equipment they have should be carried in one of the other vehicles or shared among other people.

Outriders – If your group is large and you have people to spare then you could have an outrider to each side, or if only one then to the side from which any trouble is most likely to come. Their tasks and equipment should be similar to that of the scout, but they can also be pulled in to search for and retrieve a member of the group that gets separated.

The Leader – the Leader in this context might be the leader/commander of the group, or the person who best knows the route, or if appropriate the person who has contact with the owner of the BOL to which you are headed.

The Escort/Combat Team – The job of the Escort or Combat Team is to provide backup to the Scout or Outrider if they spot or get into trouble, or to help with retrieving a member that gets separated, or to respond to any attack.

The members of this team should be the most experienced and capable you have for the task and should be armed with your most effective weaponry, whether that is guns, bows, or baseball bats. If available they should also have radios for communication between team members and with the scouts and leader.

The commander of this team should also arrange security and defence at halts, though all able bodied members of the group will take part in those tasks. If you have enough appropriate people and equipment you could put another team in the centre of The Body, near to your Diamonds.

The Body – The main part of your group follows the

Escort. In these vehicles you have the bulk of your party and equipment. At the centre of The Body you have your Principals or Diamonds i.e. your most valuable or vulnerable people and equipment, protected by all those around them.

Support Group – Near to the back of the convoy should be anyone you have who can provide mechanical or medical assistance, together with their equipment, in case a vehicle breaks down or someone becomes ill.

The Backstop – The attention of the Backstop is mainly focussed on what is behind you. They are looking for any vehicles or groups that might be following awaiting a chance to attack or relay information to others who might, either while you are on the move or at halts. This team is also part of your defence and should have next priority for any weapons.

If it is deemed necessary, this team can set up a hasty roadblock, possibly reinforced by other members of the group, to allow the main part of the convoy time to find and establish a defensive location.

When they hear that has happened, they will clear the way and allow anyone held back to pass. To prevent those people then setting up an ambush the convoy should then change route.

It is entirely possible, of course, that your convoy will consist of three people on bikes, in which case much of the above will seem to be superfluous to you. Even so, if you think about it some of the organisation and tasks would still apply. That might be Mum as Leader, kiddies as the Diamonds, and Dad as The Backstop, but the principles still hold good.

They also apply to a group on foot, though the support group might be pulling a trailer or trolley. Take a look at pictures or movies of historical conflicts such as the Napoleonic wars or US cavalry marching into Indian territory and you will see scouts or skirmishers out ahead and on either side, the officers on horses at the front of the main column, then the body of marching troops, and finally the supply wagons, followed only by a rear guard. These things track down through the years. What works, works!

Routes: - The driver/navigator of each vehicle should follow the directions, NOT the vehicle in front. That way if one vehicle goes wrong only they have to find their way back and the whole convoy does not become split.

When explaining the route it should be split into 'legs'. A leg might be an obvious stretch, such as between two towns, or along a road with a certain number, or between stopping points.

We have already covered finding routes and what to look for in doing so but one point of particular importance to note is turning places. When explaining the route, as much detail as possible should be given about turning points e.g. how far from the start of this leg or after the last village; the designation of the road onto which you are turning and to where it is signposted, and any obvious landmarks e.g. From Centre Parcs/A66, after 46.5 miles, just before the Hargill House caravan site, take Hargill to Gilling Beck/Darlington.

Spacing of vehicles/speed: - The speed of travel is generally controlled by the practical speed of the slowest vehicle or person in the group. However, the over-riding principle is that it is NEVER the responsibility of someone to keep up with the vehicle/person in front; it is always the responsibility of the person in front to maintain visual contact with the one behind them.

When you are travelling in vehicles the main points to watch for are junctions. Wherever possible a vehicle should not turn at a junction until they are sure that the one behind can see them. If traffic makes that impracticable then they should pull over as soon as possible and within sight of the junction so they can be seen by the next approaching vehicle.

While one or two vehicles might get through a junction, around a roundabout, or through traffic lights, it is common for the next to be held up. When that happens the ones that have got through pull over as soon as it is safe to do so and wait for the next to arrive behind them. For a long convoy this might have to be repeated several times with the group moving forward a way each time before all vehicles are through and can proceed.

Military convoys usually allow space between vehicles to allow other traffic a chance to overtake in stages. In war the spaces are varied so that it is more difficult for attacking aircraft or ambushers to space their gunfire or bombs. That hopefully won't be a problem for you but it certainly has been for civilians escaping conflict in some countries. Otherwise, a convoy of survivors should stay together quite closely for mutual defence and protection.

Loading of vehicles: - While the intention will always be to get everyone safely to the BOL, there is always the chance of an accident or attack that will cause the loss of one or more parts of your group.

It will be natural for members of one family to want to travel together, but for the good of them and everyone else it might be better to split them up to make best use of both vehicles and the skills some might possess. Children should be reassured that they will be reunited with their parents at halts.

If you have vehicles with the storage it also makes sense to split up resources, so that not all the fuel or food or water is in one vehicle or trailer, for example. This will probably happen naturally, with families wanting to keep control of their own stuff even though they might be willing to share if someone is short of something or to put into the pot for communal cooking.

If you have spare space in the passenger area of vehicles then it makes sense to pack some with goods, on the nearside especially, both to make use of that space and to provide some protection for the people.

Vehicles should be loaded logically, with items not likely to be required until you reach the BOL put in first and vehicle tools or other items that might be needed en route at the back, on top, or otherwise easy to access. Fuel should also be at the back but at floor level so that any leakage doesn't spoil other items.

The load should then be covered and non-attractive routine things such as bedding scattered on top so that the good stuff is not visible to pedestrians or passing vehicles.

Protection on the move: – Although your chosen route should keep you clear of the mass of refugees, you might still face attack from some who have been sensible enough to avoid the main roads but are desperate for anything they can get from you.

This is a situation you must discuss with the other people in your group, to try and identify who you can rely on to fight if necessary.

You can never be sure of the response from people who have not been in the situation before. Some will declare themselves to be a veritable attack dog but when the situation arises turn out to be a fluffy puppy. Mums who say they could never raise a hand will turn green and burst out of their blouses if their children's foodstuffs are threatened. If you are lucky you might have a veteran or two who has been and done. All you can do is make the best judgement you can and hope the chosen will respond well if called upon.

Having identified those who you believe will be useful in defence you must organise them and position them in appropriate places in the order of travel. These teams become your combat groups and a more military structure is appropriate for them. Each team must have a designated commander and each of the members an allocated role according to their skills and capabilities.

If you have any former soldiers in the group use them as advisors and based on that input then allow the teams to discuss and sort out their own tactics. You aren't going to turn people with no military experience into soldiers in ten minutes, however many sessions of Call of Duty they have played on their games console, or paintballs or plastic BBs they have fired at their mates. Neither will there be any time for anyone with real experience to provide detailed training for the others. Do what you can.

If any have real guns, the owners will not want to give them up, but if they aren't already in the hands of those best able to use them you should try to show the logic of them being so. You probably won't succeed but try anyway.

You should also discuss what your reaction will be if people recognise that you are prepared and better off than they are and approach you asking for help. If you are on the move it is easier. Keep all doors locked as you go and beware of people at the roadside begging for help, they could be bandits trying to ambush or hijack you. Watch them closely without appearing to do so and just keep going.

Dark windows on a car help to hide the contents but scream 'posh' to many people and might make you a target. There is nothing you can do about it if that is what you've got but bear it in mind if you are considering what to get as a BOV.

It might seem very 'Mad Max' but if there is a danger from rioters or looters, do consider covering windows with wire mesh to make it harder for anyone to break in to steal your supplies or vehicle or simply to attack you. In the early stages of a disaster and among other evacuees it might make you stand out, but once you are clear of the crowd that shouldn't be a worry and a more assertive defensive posture is worthwhile.

If I was writing this for other countries there is a lot more I might add to this section, but for a UK centred book let's leave it at that for now.

Halts: – Whatever mode of transport they are using, people on the move have to stop eventually, to drink, eat, pee, poo, and/or rest.

How soon and how often you stop will depend on how you are travelling, how long the intended journey is, and the condition of the people in the group

If you are walking you might want to schedule a brief stop, say five or ten minutes, per hour. If the members of the group are in good condition you could get some miles behind you and not have the first stop until the end of the second hour and then break each hour after that. Then you can have a longer break after 4 hours to eat, drink, talk about how it is going, refresh yourselves for the next leg, and make any adjustments to pace or other arrangements.

If someone has to stop outside of scheduled halts, perhaps because stress has got the better of their insides, then it is simpler to arrange if you can simply talk to one another. Communication is easier and somebody having a quick nip into the bushes isn't a great problem.

Because you are not putting out so much energy, travelling by bike, horse, or light boat might require less frequent stops but that does depend on how fit and practised people are and the nature of the terrain over which you are moving.

If a passenger in a car or other wheeled transport knows they have a problem, and they cannot travel where they have some privacy, try to put them in with people of similar age and sex who will be sympathetic. Provide a suitable receptacle - even a bucket might do - and tissues and wipes as required.

However, more important than when or how often you stop is where you do so.

Assuming that there is a threat of any kind from other people, you need to ensure that your stopping place provides you with the best security you can find. It doesn't matter how you are travelling or whether you are in an urban or rural area, the basic requirements are the same. To that end, your halts should provide:

Cover from view – if other people see a group gathered and particularly if they can see that you are eating, drinking, have shelter, and seem secure, they may either want to join you or steal from you.

Although there is some safety in numbers, you might not have the supplies or transport to be able to take on additional people, and even if you could your BOL might not be able to accommodate them. You also don't know what problems they might bring with them or cause you on the way. Unless you are very well provided it is therefore better to avoid the situation arising.

There are also those who might see you, who would be more inclined to attack than beg, either in a direct assault or by approaching and demanding that you share what you have, 'because they haven't got anything and it is only right that you should give them some of what you've got'.

That sense of entitlement is only too prevalent in our society and refusal will almost certainly provoke anger and possibly violence unless you can show that they have no chance. If you do that they are likely to try to either gather others then attack in force or destroy what you have, rather than let you have something they want but can't have.

You should look for somewhere that allows you some freedom to move around, where any fires or other lights you use will be concealed, where noises you make are not magnified, and smells are quickly dispersed.

Protection from attack - look for limited routes of access but also an escape path for you if you need it. You want solid ground or objects around you that will stop any missiles, be it stones thrown or fired from a catapult, or petrol bombs, to arrows or even gunfire. Do not allow anyone to get above you, because the high ground always gives an advantage, whether it is up a hill or a higher level in a building.

While being hidden from sight you should have points of observation from which you can spot anybody approaching and challenge or attack them if you have to.

Your defence/combat team should be searching for somewhere that has as many as possible of these features whenever you are looking to make a halt, even if that is a brief rest stop but especially if it is a longer halt.

You should post lookouts/sentries to warn you of any threat and everyone must be ready to respond if the alert is raised. Parents and grandparents make good sentries if their offspring are in the group, because they are very aware that they have something precious to protect. If the stop is a long one, put sentries in pairs and stagger their shifts, so that one person is on for an hour, another starting at the same time is on for two. After an hour a new person replaces one and at the end of two hours someone else replaces the other that started the system. In that way you always have one person out of the pair who has been on shift for no more than an hour.

Arrange the length of shifts according to how tired people are and bearing in mind the weather. If you have to use drivers as guards, try to give them early or late shifts so that they get the maximum period of continuous rest, for the safety of everyone in their vehicle.

If you have very limited numbers in the group, work the 'buddy system'. In this method one person sleeps while the other stands watch and wakes their buddy when it is time to change shift. Unless pairs are disciplined or the threat is clear and imminent this is quite a dangerous system as the chances of the one on watch dozing off is quite high.

To help your sentries, there is a variety of remote warning devices you can buy or improvise, ranging from military issue trip flares, to alarm mines fitted with blank cartridges, to PIR activated lights, or audible or silent alarms, to tin cans on a piece of string, or gravel, broken glass or dry branches and twigs that are perhaps less obvious but which will still alert you to someone approaching. If you are feeling aggressive, many of the triggers used for these can, instead, be attached to booby traps. Or, of course, you might have dogs that will serve to give you warning and possibly act as defenders too.

Whenever you do stop, you should unload as little as possible and reload things as soon as you have finished using them, to allow a quick exit if necessary. If someone wants to go off in search of privacy to attend to bodily functions they should always be accompanied. If two need the same thing, one attends to their needs while the other keeps watch and then they swap roles.

Opportunity to resupply - most importantly with water. Don't assume the quality of water in an emergency, whatever the source always treat it as potentially suspect. Even if you have good reserves you should never pass up a chance to replenish any consumables you use, you never know when or if you will get another chance.

There may be times when you have to stop at a place not of your choosing, due to one of the situations covered in Actions On for example. If that happens, you have to use the best position you can, deploy security and otherwise keep most people onboard ready to move as quickly as possible. More details for various events are explained in the AO paragraphs.

Above all, recognise that halts are vulnerable times and anything you can do to improve your protection is always worthwhile.

Lights

Lights can be friends or foes, depending on how you use them. They can show you the way and reveal threats while to some extent hiding you from enemies but they can also give away your position when other people would not otherwise have known you were there. They can also be used for signalling if you don't have two-way radios for communication.

Because of the increased danger of travelling when it is dark and of announcing by using lights that you are doing so, you should seriously consider whether it is necessary or whether you should halt for the night.

On clear moonlit nights it is possible to drive in many conditions without using lights. That is particularly useful during your final approaches to a BOL or rest place.

One of the problems in an emergency is that we are used to living in a world of light, where at any time most of our surroundings are, or can be, as bright as or brighter than during the day. A disaster often alters that, putting out streetlights and most of those within buildings. That can increase even further the fears of those not used to being in the dark.

Another issue is that most people are not used to living under threat and having to hide from predators. Until they have experienced the consequences of a lack of discipline they will not believe it.

Those in denial and older children especially, will be deliberately disobedient, not understanding the danger their actions can cause and how far their light can be seen in otherwise dark surroundings. You might not be able to totally prevent it, but it is a hazard of which you and other responsible group members should be aware.

Light signals should be kept simple, limited in scope, and agreed in advance so that everyone knows how and when to use them. You might want to use them for identification, to signal a vehicle ahead to stop, or other urgent messages relevant to your group.

Actions on:
Blocked route
If you have a scout out in front of the main group it can save you from many inconveniences and possibly from serious danger. The scout should operate as far ahead as reliable communication will allow. That gives the main group chance to respond before they enter a danger area or to find a suitable place to turn if an alternative route is needed.

If the call to stop is caused by blockage due to an accident, damage to the road or fallen trees or masonry, the escort group should go forward to join the scout in order to assess whether the blockage is passable, possibly after some clearance, or if a detour will be required. This will vary according to the vehicles and equipment you have e.g. a heavy truck, tow ropes, chain saw, etc.

SOPs for brief halts apply. Deliberate blockages are dealt with below.
Breakdown

In the event of one vehicle breaking down, initially the whole group should stop. If you have anybody experienced in maintenance of the type of transport involved then they should be brought into play.

If the decision is that it cannot be fixed with the resources and facilities you have available then you have to decide whether to tow the disabled vehicle or redistribute its passengers and other contents and then abandon it. If you are going to tow, you might want to lighten the load by spreading some of it about anyway. SOPs for brief halts apply.

Separation

If the driver of any vehicle realises that the one that should be behind them is missing, perhaps after a turning, they should stop as soon as practicable, after signalling by whatever means is available to the vehicle ahead that they are going to do so.

If a vehicle behind another sees that it has missed a turning, the driver of the following vehicle should signal if possible but otherwise make the turn and stick to the agreed route.

When someone realises that they now have none of their group ahead of or behind them, they should stop as soon as it is safe to do so, work out where they have gone wrong, and if they can determine that turn around and head back to re-join the convoy, confident in the knowledge that the others will be waiting for them for as long as is reasonable.

When they re-join the others they should slip back into their usual place in the line. If the occupants of the vehicle can't work out what has happened then they should find a safe place, visible from the road/track they were on, look to their own security and wait until the scout, escort, or outrider comes to find them and guide them back to the fold.

Official roadblock

If you don't have any advance warning and you come up against an official roadblock the only sensible response is polite compliance with whatever instructions you are given.

The chances are good that those manning the roadblock will be better armed than you and have open communication with their operations centre, though that might differ with whether it is a police or military position.

Official roadblocks are usually sited where there is little warning of their presence until it is too late for a vehicle to avoid them. This is often after a bend in the road and if the block functions in both directions then an S bend is preferred. Exactly where that will be depends on their function.

If it is to block a particular route, the position will be sited where there is access to an alternative way or sufficient room for vehicles to turn and go back the way they came. If it is to stop and confine people trying to leave a zone it will be where they can divert you into a holding area for 'processing'. Or it might be a check point, where the intention is to identify those who are moving, where they are going, and quite possibly to confiscate certain classes of possessions, potentially including firearms, communication equipment, medical supplies, food, and fuel, according to the nature of the emergency.

Both police and military roadblocks will have a barrier, possibly vehicles, part of which can be moved if you are allowed to proceed, maybe as a solid barrier or sometimes forming a chicane, and a spiked chain or other method of disabling any vehicle that tries to break through.

A military roadblock usually has 'Stops' placed some distance either side of the barrier. These are positions, often equipped with a machine gun or sniper rifle, placed to stop vehicles that do detect the block from turning back or otherwise escaping. They are not normally more than one hundred metres or so away from the barrier but it does depend on the road layout.

Their orders or 'rules of engagement' will vary in accordance with the situation. If a vehicle tries to flee they might just note its registration number and other physical details so it can be stopped later, they might try to disable the vehicle, or they could try to shoot the driver and passengers.

The latter choice would most often only be considered appropriate if the occupants of the vehicle opened fire first or were identified as wanted people the block was intended to catch.

If you have several vehicles in your group then as soon as the first one spots the roadblock it should signal that to the one behind it, which should then stop. What you do then depends on whether it is a police or military block and if the lead vehicle is the first in line to be stopped or behind a queue. If it is first there is little choice but to slowly approach the block and go through the process while the second vehicle hangs back to see what happens and respond accordingly. If there is a line you might decide to try turning back or reversing, but if it is a military block remember what is in the preceding paragraphs.

Official roadblocks are bad news for Preppers bugging out and you should do whatever you can to detect and avoid them before being stopped.

Unofficial roadblock

Unofficial roadblocks are even worse news than official ones and can be far more dangerous. They might be placed simply to stop you proceeding into an area or through a village where the inhabitants don't want any outsiders bringing disease or looking for handouts.

They might be there to rob you of anything the blockers want or even everything you have, vehicles and all. The people manning the block might not be as well equipped as police or soldiers but they will certainly be less disciplined and more prone to violence.

How you deal with being stopped by a block of this sort is down to how solidly it is put together, how heavily it is manned, how well you are equipped and armed, and how brave or desperate you are.

The safest and most sensible option is to avoid it, turn back and find a way around, anything else is almost certainly going to see someone of one side or the other, or both, hurt or killed.

That is only justifiable if not getting through is going to cause the death of some, or all, of your group anyway.

If possible, then rather than trying to drive through, which the block will be specifically designed to prevent, and if you have part of your group that is armed, dismount, manoeuvre, and attack the block from the side or rear.

Each of your vehicles should have a driver in place and as soon as you have driven off the people manning the block, some of the combat group should stand guard while others clear a path and then the vehicles proceed, picking up the combatants as they go.

Be under no illusions, attempting something like this is a desperate measure only to be undertaken if there is no acceptable alternative. Friends and neighbours are probably going to be seriously hurt and some might die. Members of your group, who might never have been in a fight using anything more deadly than their fists, might have to kill. That will affect them forever afterwards.

I wouldn't even suggest or mention it if I hadn't seen it needed and done by civilians in other countries. Sometimes they were successful.

In two places we came across, some time after the battle, they were not and as far as we could make out every member of the group that had been stopped was killed. In one of those incidents all the women, children and elderly had been executed at the side of the road. Whenever there is any other way, ALWAYS avoid conflict while bugging out. Your intention is to survive. Getting killed on the way does not meet the aim!

There are many other situations you for which might see the need to make preparations and discuss response. An attack of any sort on your group always gives you three options: fight, flee, or surrender.

Which you take is down to you and the people with you. If ever you face those choices, may everything that is good be with you.

Support:

Special equipment, supplies and skills: the more of these that you have in your group, the better your chances. Of particular help in most Bug Out situations are mechanics, medics, and soldiers, but many other skills can be of use too and more so when you reach your BOL. If you are prepping, develop your group with Bug Out needs in mind as well as those essential skills you will need after you reach your BOL.

Feeding and water: If your move takes more than a few hours you will definitely need to drink and eat to maintain your health and energy. If you are using physical exertion in bugging out, regular water intake is vital. Start out with as copious a supply as you can carry and resupply at any opportunity.

When you stop there are always lots of tasks to be done, so communal cooking and feeding is more efficient. All parties within the group should contribute, and share in the feeding. Unless someone is ill and eating would be pointless, everyone should take on nourishment in order to stay strong. More importantly everyone should drink, even if you are issuing rations and ensuring that they drink what they are given.

Signals:

Lights: I have already mentioned using headlights for signalling between vehicles but you can also use them to identify members of your party. A piece of transparent, coloured film over one headlight, or part of it, can make it easier for those within the group to distinguish between a vehicle that is one of yours and one of a similar model and colour that is not.

If it is safe to use light but not noise, then signals from torches can also be used. Most often this is done for identification as a form of password, with one sequence used to challenge and a different one to respond.

Sound: vehicle horns can be used for signalling but on the move there is always a chance that they won't be heard, especially when vehicles are heavily loaded and all windows are shut. However, horns, whistles, or other loud noises can be used to sound an alarm, especially at halts if you have been discovered and therefore making noise is irrelevant.

Radios: the most useful form of signalling, however, is the use of two-way radios. PMR radios have limited range but are extremely cheap, easily available, simple to operate and require no external network, as mobile phones do. Their limited range can be an advantage as your messages are less likely to be overheard by people outside of your group and yet it is quite adequate for vehicle to vehicle travelling close together.

There are lots of different makes and models available, with varying features and correspondingly differing prices. Some use standard batteries such as AA or AAA, some recharge from either vehicles or the mains. If yours is a mains charger you can always use an inverter to run it from a vehicle. If you are not using motor vehicles then the standard battery models are more appropriate.

Vehicle mount and handheld CBs are still available. They tend to be more expensive than the PMRs but similarly do not require a licence and model can be had that use any of the power sources employed by the smaller radios. The big advantages of CB are longer range than PMR – better, for example, between lead vehicle/escort and scouts or outriders – and a greater range of frequencies. CB is not as popular in the UK as it used to be, so there are usually channels free of any other users.

And finally there is HF/VHF shortwave. These have the potential for very long range with a suitable antenna and are available as base station, vehicle mount, or handheld models. They are the most expensive of the three civilian types but handhelds are still available for under £50.

You do, however, need a licence to transmit and must attend a course and sit an exam to get the licence and your unique callsign. The exam is simple at Foundation level, which is all you really need for these purposes. In fact, although regular use is always good to take maximum benefit from your investment and develop competence, you don't need the licence to buy the kit and its relevance in the aftermath of a disaster that required you to Bug Out is debateable. Not that I would ever recommend or suggest that you should ever break the law, of course.

Summary

Even in normal times there are dangers of which we should all be aware and for which we should be prepared. In an emergency that demands a bug-out, when disorganisation and disorientation result in a disruption of the usual rules of law and behaviour, those threats can be magnified to a massive degree.

Whether you are travelling alone, as part of a small team, or with a larger group, remember:

Plan your move with a variety of options in mind and be flexible in which you use as the situation develops

Choose a route that is least likely to be used by others and that you are confident you can complete using your chosen mode of movement. Reconnoitre and test it.

Establish caches if appropriate and practicable.

Know the dangers you might face while on the move and how to counter them

Know the dangers you might face at halts and how to counter them

Plan your journey. Ensure everyone in the group knows what their role is, how and where they will travel, what is expected of them given the resources available, and what support they can call on.

Have methods of communications that meet the needs of your group and ensure everyone knows how to use them and what various signals mean

If possible, practise people their role and how to respond to various situations they might encounter.

Summary

This is a book intended to provide information that will be of help to civilians who have to Bug Out from their home due to the effects of an emergency or disaster.

I have tried to cover a wide range of situations that you might encounter, from ones affecting only your own family to others that might be of national or global proportions.

I have done my best to make it applicable to UK citizens, because most of the other books on the market are primarily written for other areas.

It is aimed at skills and resources available to most inhabitants of these islands, but inevitably, because some of the situations are so similar to those familiar to the armed forces, some of the information, and especially the last chapter, might seem rather militaristic. I can't apologise for that; the reality of bugging out from a major disaster, in times when the government and its agencies are disorganised and not in total control, through threats from various desperate or avaricious people, puts you in situations many a soldier would recognise.

I have also included some references to my own experiences that are relevant to the subject. They aren't always pleasant but they are there to give you a taste of what the reality of these situations can be like. If they distress you, I'm sorry, the memories aren't comfortable for me either but if they help to prepare you for what might be to come, then that is the purpose of the book and I hope that it might help you in that.

Acknowledgements

I would like to thank the people who so generously offered their assistance during the writing of this book. Their participation helped it become a work I can hope all my readers will enjoy but never need.

In particular, my thanks go to my wife Patricia, for putting up with my early mornings and late nights with my eyes and mind focussed only on my computer screen while walls went unpainted and fittings unfixed.

And to my friends Tim and Jason from the Ludlow Survivors Group for their invaluable help with proofing and suggestions, and Chris for expert guidance on all things boat related; a big Thank You, to you all.

Useful References

Streetcraft - the Ludlow Survival Group guide to Urban Survival, Preparedness and Response
 http://www.lulu.com/shop/ludlow-survivors-group/streetcraft/paperback/product-20590304.html
The UK government National Risk Register of Civil Emergencies – information on what government advisors think is likely to affect the UK, how, and what they and you can do about it.
http://www.cabinetoffice.gov.uk/resource-library/national-risk-register

About the author

Son of a Scottish mother and Yorkshire father, David Eric Crossley was raised in Yorkshire. After a number of unsatisfying jobs, he joined the forces in 1970 and was a soldier for over 20 years.

Qualified as an instructor in Nuclear Biological and Chemical Warfare, Combat Survival, Urban and Counter-revolutionary Warfare, Signals, Advanced First Aid, Light Rescue and Fire fighting, among other things, he served in Africa, Asia, the Gulf, Central and South America and Europe. He has lived through the reality and aftermath of wars and counter-terrorist operations, and as an advisor and rescuer during Aid to the Civil Powers missions after major disasters overseas.

After leaving the forces, David settled in Scotland. He worked as Training Manager Scotland for the British Red Cross for 4 years including training overseas service and emergency response volunteers, and now works as an independent survival consultant and writer.

David has been writing professionally since the 1980s and has had over 100 magazine articles and short stories published in outdoors, survival, military, business and general interest magazines. He has also published Bugging In – a guide to survival-in-place; Bugging In and Bugging Out - in a single volume; compiled, edited and wrote much of an urban survival reference, published as Streetcraft, for Ludlow Survivors Group; plus There Falls No Shadow - the first novel of a post-apocalyptic series; and is working on the second in the series, Slow the Shadow Creeps. All are available in print from CreateSpace or for Kindle from the Amazon Kindle store.

Check out David's website at: http://www.tfns.co.uk
David welcomes feedback from readers of his work. Please
email him at: books@decrossley.co.uk
Twitter @TfnsbooksDavid
Facebook David E. Crossley Books

Also by this author:
Bugging In - a UK centred guide to Survival-in-Place
Bugging In and Bugging Out – Bugging In and Bugging Out
in a single volume
There Falls No Shadow – a post-apocalyptic novel, first in the
Shadows trilogy
Streetcraft – an urban survival guide for the UK. With
contributions from other members of Ludlow Survival Group.

www.ingramcontent.com/pod-product-compliance
Lightning Source LLC
Chambersburg PA
CBHW070700290526
45790CB00001B/396